PRAISE FOR

Floating in a Most Peculiar Way

New York Times Editors' Choice
Amazon Editors' Pick

"Herein lies the beauty of *Floating in a Most Peculiar Way:* it reveals how we carry trauma with us, how that trauma can cause us to hurt one another, and how we still love and carry one another with wounds unhealed . . . These are words in which those of us who have floated outside for so long can touch down for a bit, and connect."
— Ijeoma Oluo, *New York Times Book Review*

"A beautifully told story about displacement and coming of age."
— *People*

"Stupendous doesn't even begin to describe the extraordinary power and exhilarating beauty of *Floating in a Most Peculiar Way.* Here is a memoir that blazes like a star and rhymes like Paul Beatty at his best. Louis Chude-Sokei is a writer with all the gifts and then some."
— Junot Díaz, author of the Pulitzer Prize–winning *The Brief Wondrous Life of Oscar Wao* and of *This Is How You Lose Her*

"Chude-Sokei chronicles his . . . missteps, advances, and inner conflicts to create a moving, perspicacious account of disguising his origins, of adopting pose after pose, of seeking acceptance. It is a story of perplexed identity, of its permutations and specificities."
— *Minneapolis Star Tribune*

"Storytelling, Chude-Sokei realized early, is 'an act of survival.' Here, he writes himself into existence — his abandonment; his less-than-othering; his search for manhood among interchangeable aunties; answers to his past; his return to his birthplace. Ending where he began, he comes full circle toward luminous acceptance. Readers are guaranteed an extraordinary journey . . . an exquisite memoir."
— *Shelf Awareness*

"From the start it is clear *Floating in a Most Peculiar Way* is going to be a journey of discovery like few others . . . This is narrative storytelling at its best."
— *New York Journal of Books*

"Chude-Sokei's *Floating in a Most Peculiar Way* is a rich, immersive coming-of-age tale from a man of eccentric, transnational upbringing. Chude-Sokei's honest and eloquent writing ultimately transforms his memoir into a superlative and unforgettable book."
— Chigozie Obioma, author of the Booker Prize finalists
The Fishermen and *An Orchestra of Minorities*

"This is autobiography at its best. In stories of the multiple blended accents, atrocities, musics, prejudices, and foods of London, Biafra, Jamaica, DC, South Central LA, and elsewhere, Chude-Sokei confronts the nightmare of history — along with the persistent, sometimes joyful adventure of awakening from it."
— Robert Pinsky, poet laureate of the
United States, 1997–2000

"*Floating in a Most Peculiar Way* delivers a riveting immigrant's journey spanning the African diaspora that is certain to refine our sense of what it means to be American, and to complicate, especially, what it means to be a Black American."
— Charles Johnson, author of the National Book Award–
winning *Middle Passage* and of *The Way of the Writer:
Reflections on the Art and Craft of Storytelling*

"An affecting memoir of life as an exile, with a David Bowie soundtrack in the background . . . Deftly profound."
— *Kirkus Reviews*, starred review

"Absorbing . . . Highly recommended for all memoir readers."
— *Booklist*

"A beautiful, plainspoken work . . . This hard-to-put-down memoir both enlightens and inspires."
— *Publishers Weekly*

*Floating
in a
Most
Peculiar
Way*

LOUIS CHUDE-SOKEI

Floating
in a
Most
Peculiar
Way

MARINER BOOKS

Boston · *New York*

First Mariner Books edition 2022
marinerbooks.com

Designed by Chloe Foster

Library of Congress Cataloging-in-Publication Data has been applied for.
ISBN 9780358639701 (trade paper)
ISBN 9781328781079 (e-book)
ISBN 9780358395027 (audio)

1 2021
4500844650

Portions of chapters "Space Oddity" and "Heroes" first appeared, in different form, in *Hambone* No. 20 published in 2012. Portions of chapters "Life on Mars" and "African Night Flight" first published, in different form, in the November 2013 issue of the *Chimurenga Chronic*.

For Adaorah.

This is where you begin.

Contents

PROLOGUE: FUTURE LEGEND   ix

1. Space Oddity   1

2. Heroes   29

3. Life on Mars   42

4. Suffragette City   60

5. Absolute Beginners (Part I)   80

6. All the Young Dudes   86

7. We Are the Dead   103

8. This Is Not America   124

9. Young Americans   152

10. Absolute Beginners (Part II)   163

11. African Night Flight   182

12. The Man Who Fell to Earth   207

ACKNOWLEDGMENTS   221

Prologue

FUTURE LEGEND

In my mother and father's time, "exile" would have been the description for people like us. It was a sexy word in some circles. The common terms now are "immigrant" or "refugee." Neither of those have the same appeal. They come laden with a sense of political inconvenience or victimization. And they imply that the place you have come from still exists.

Throughout my childhood, my mother told me that we were from a country that had disappeared or been "killed." The murder of our country was a crime she would never forgive because not only had she become a citizen of that country, but she and my father had been partly responsible for its invention. Sometimes our country had been "starved to death." Our enemy, the Federal Republic of Nigeria, had identified starvation as a legitimate tactic of war and deployed it against us with some virtuosity. We'd become famous for our hunger, particularly our children, who became celebrities in what many called Africa's first televised war. But we weren't exiles because nobody owed us anything. We were immigrants because back in my mother's day that term implied that we were needed in whatever country we ended up in.

Nobody felt guilty for our country's disappearance because it hadn't survived long enough to appear on any official maps. It was more than a rumor but had not become a symbol. A handful of African nations had recognized it, and Israel and a few European countries had supported it without providing official recognition. Though virtually forgotten, there were still traces of our country in the lexicon of global charity. For example, it existed in tragic photos of emaciated babies with swollen heads and stomachs. As I said, we'd become famous for our hunger. Images of our children introduced kwashiorkor to the world, a disease so cruel as to be ironic: extreme hunger made the stomach expand enough to suggest gluttony.

We were from Biafra, mind you. *Not* Nigeria. My mother was

emphatic about the distinction. The latter was just a placeholder, a country that was to our real homeland as a scar is to a wound. In other words, it was just like me, as I was to my father who was killed just months before his beloved country was. His death, many said, precipitated the end. Most of what I knew about him when I was a boy came from the endless recollections of those eager to hold on to that almost country. Some say he was its light, its grace, a reason to justify a cultural penchant for song. But when he was gone, all that was left was bloodshed and his people did not sing about death. This was certainly how it was for his family, many of whom were soldiers also; and his village; and his ethnic group, the Igbos. So it was for his wife — a Jamaican woman who had migrated to England to help rebuild the colonial motherland after World War II and then migrated again to West Africa just weeks after meeting him.

Nigerians may not have accepted her initially as African, and her husband's people might not have accepted her as Igbo. But *Biafra,* that was something else. Biafra didn't have the luxury to discriminate within its tender borders, and in it she'd been as heroic as any man or any African. And her son, she claimed, was the first Biafra baby. She'd say this even after I'd gotten old enough to decide that it was meaningless, since we'd left so early in my life. The war was declared on July 6, 1967. I was born just past midnight of that day. Family legend had it that while she was in labor she could hear the first fruits of the federal government's bombing campaign against Biafra, and when she'd given birth, there had been word of casualties nearby.

I don't remember Biafra or leaving it. Apparently, all I had with me when I arrived in Jamaica was a song, not an Igbo song but a Western one played on the radio about floating in space and choosing never to come down. It was a song about someone named Major Tom, and it eventually became my only memory of my origins in Africa. My mother told me I first heard it in Gabon, the country we'd fled to just before the final collapse when there were too many dead to still call Biafra a country. She said one of the aid workers played and sang the song often, and that it soothed me to sleep. She claimed that the aid worker's name was Tom and that he must have been a major like my father, but that stretched credulity.

I remember none of this, but I do remember the first time I heard the word "Biafra." It was also the first time I remember meeting an African other than myself.

I must have been five or six years old. My mother had returned to America in the wake of my Jamaican grandmother's death, and I'd been adopted by family friends who were members of a rigidly orthodox Seventh-day Adventist community in Montego Bay.

The plan was for my mother to send for me once she'd established herself in America with work and a home, and had managed all the paperwork necessary for my border crossing. Jamaica is where I began to hunt for that song in order to verify a past before that desperate island.

*Floating
in a
Most
Peculiar
Way*

Space Oddity

My first African arrived while I was chasing Cousin Cecil around the backyard with a gun fashioned out of hardened coconut-tree fronds. He had given the fronds to me in trade for the map of a sunken continent I'd torn from either a comic book or one of the science fiction novels I had to smuggle into the house because they were forbidden.

Cousin Cecil was the adopted son of the matriarch and patriarch of this home for left-behind children, Big Auntie and Uncle Daddy. Big Auntie was a high-ranking administrator for the Seventh-day Adventist churches on our side of the island. She was as large in physique as she was in authority and volume. She was in-famous for her belches, thunderous affirmations of power. Small and wiry, Uncle Daddy was infamous for his wicked laughter, which came even when delivering punishment. He owned and operated a tour bus, a Japanese-made vehicle rare in those days, the pride of the household and their church. Like everyone in a country like Jamaica, Big Auntie and Uncle Daddy were involved in multiple other businesses and schemes to keep their large household afloat. Uncle Daddy was a driver but also a contractor, a builder, a fisherman, a mechanic. That's why the backyard we were running through was perilous and wonderful, dense with the detritus of his many professional failures and successes.

Cousin Cecil was the Two-Gun Kid to my alter ego, the dark and driven Phantom, also known as the Ghost Who Walks. My cousin's unknown Middle Eastern origins meant his skin was far closer to white than anyone we knew. He was famous for his abil-ity to shimmy up lean and tall palm trees, hand over hand like a bug-eyed yellow monkey. The Phantom always struggled to climb those trees, his hands too tender for the rough bark. This time I cut him off from the nearest tree, cornering him against a wall near a glassy pool of oil where two car engines sat exposed like the entrails of prehistoric beasts, which we all agreed they were.

Suddenly, he bolted toward the doghouse under the mango

tree. According to our laws, he would be granted sanctuary there. Before I could head him off, I heard our names called from the front of the house. My name was first, which meant I was the primary concern, though it was rare for only one of us to be punished even if only one of us was guilty. We marched through the long central hallway that led from the backyard past the house girls' room, through the kitchen, the dining room, and into the parlor at the front where worship services were held. Hortense, the main house girl (a woman, really, almost as old as Big Auntie) lumbered knock-kneed against the doorway that led into the parlor. The smell of cooking grease was on her hands, which tenderly and invisibly grazed my shoulder. It was a sign that everything was all right.

Everyone in the house was there. I specifically remember three of Big Auntie and Uncle Daddy's four daughters, and two other girl cousins rooming for the school year. Hortense stood next to another house girl with Big Auntie, Uncle Daddy, and I'm sure one of the guest missionaries they regularly hosted from Loma Linda, the Seventh-day Adventist university in America. Surrounding us all in the room that suddenly seemed a courtroom was the inevitable tribe of children that comprised my primary community in that house, whose parents had *gone a foreign,* be it to Canada, England, or America. Sitting against the far wall with the two house dogs at her feet was Grandma—and it was never clear if she was Big Auntie's or Uncle Daddy's mother — her hair recalling the powdered wig of a High Court judge. The imagery was complete.

Before I could wonder about the stranger, he leaped from his seat and rushed violently at me. He was a tall, extremely dark man with flat features whose skin seemed to be shining not from perspiration but due to its own sheen. Had there been no other boys present, I would have shrieked. His multicolored fabric billowed as he descended. I remained frozen. The shiny man fell to his knees, grabbing and shaking my shoulders.

"Is this the boy? Is this *him?*"

He looked at Big Auntie, who nodded.

"Yes. Oh, yes. *This* is the boy. I can see his father very well . . . you don't have to tell me."

Looking around at the audience, the shiny man addressed them in an accent that tightened the back of my throat.

"God is wonderful. God is great. This is *his* son . . . *the first son of the first son.*"

He paused with an expression that suggested incredulity at the fact that the onlookers did not know who I was. He then began once again to vigorously shake the child who was apparently *the* boy.

"You know who you are, boy? Do you know yourself?"

What kind of question was that to ask any child?

He pronounced my name in a way I'd never heard before. There were many more syllables.

"You are the son of the major and are named after him. One of the heroes of Biafra! Your father was the right hand of the great general, the man who led us, the first Biafra head of state, Odumegwu Ojukwu!"

This was the first time I was told that my father was famous and that we had been in a war, and the first time that I heard Ojukwu's name. It was also the first time I heard the phrase that would repeat itself for years, "the first son of the first son." I'd simply thought that I was treated as I was because of where I'd come from. I was, after all, on an island and in a household that had largely negative associations with the idea of Africa.

The African surveyed the surrounding crowd. His brow furrowed as if he expected the others to join in his disbelief that I couldn't answer his questions. Cousin Mark, who was destined for Canada, furrowed his own brow in disgust or maybe jealousy. If it was the latter, it was due to the attention I was getting, not to the revelation of nobility. Cousin June the Younger began to giggle at my stupidity. She tugged at the skirt of Cousin June the Older, who may have been shaking her head in disbelief. Both of them were headed to England, and their mother sent things down for them far more frequently than anyone else's. Our parents — mothers, actually, it was always mothers — sent remittances for our upkeep and education, and occasionally barrels loaded with clothes, toys, and gifts. These things rarely found their way into our hands. They were deemed too valuable for children in a country like that, and for Big Auntie, foreign products reeked of some distant sin. But just knowing that these packages would come gave each of us value in the house, and we were ranked accordingly, so the arrogance of both Cousins June was warranted.

The Two-Gun Kid had vanished, forcing Cousin Cecil to make sense of what was happening to me without his mask. I had a need to see Cousin Violet. When things made no sense, it was always helpful to look to her, not for clarity but to gauge her comfort with the confusion. Cousin Violet (also destined for Canada) was sitting behind two of the older girls and staring quizzically into her palm as if nothing unusual was going on. Her mouth was open, her eyes tightened, and her legs spread so wide apart that she would no doubt soon be hit by one of the older girls.

"You must know this always," the shiny man said, lips flaking with white speckles that stood out against his dark skin. "You are the son of the greatest one of our people. A hero. You must know yourself. We are Biafran and we will fight. The battle may be lost but never the war. They assassinated your father, a great, great man, and sent us all everywhere, everyplace. But you are him in spirit. The general is in exile, but this is not cowardice or giving up for lost. Never mind what you will read in the newspapers and the books they will write. We have not failed. This condition is not forever and not permanent because no condition is. No condition is permanent is something our people say, your people. *No condition is permanent!* Are you hearing me?"

Cousin Cecil was cowering against Hortense's long bent legs and scarred bare feet. She never wore shoes except to funerals and church on Saturday mornings, which meant that her feet were calloused to a hardness that was close to leather in texture. It seemed she could walk across any surface.

"You must know who you are always," the man continued. "You are an Igbo boy, an Igbo boy, an *I*-gbo boy and this is not your home. You are not Jamaican. Biafra is your home! You are the son of the greatest Onitsha man. A handsome *handsomest* man, tall and fair like a white man but with pure African blood. The general said he was the one who decided to call our country Biafra — yes, *your father.* Oh, I used to see his car up and down the road from Awka to Enugu. BAF1 was the license plate. He was Biafra Air Force number 1 because he made and commanded our air force. You must learn all these things and tell our story. Do not forget these things no matter how long you stay in this place. Are you hearing me?"

By now even more children, including some from the neighborhood and our church, had emerged from the various parts of the house and were watching from the edges of the parlor. They stood alongside the house girls, hair half-oiled and half-plaited, foreheads glistening. Cousin Brenda (destined for New York) hit Cousin Violet quietly but firmly. Cousin Violet's legs closed abruptly but her eyes remained fixed on her palm and her wet mouth was wide open.

"This is the boy. I can *not* believe this thing. God is truly great. Your mother is a great woman. Because of what she has done, what we were is possible again. She saved many lives. Oh, the children . . . she took many of our children to Gabon and saved them. And you, you will one day return and take your place. That is how the story must end. Are you hearing me?"

There was a sudden dizziness as my past was revealed in a way that only adventure novels and comics had so far suggested as possible narratives. A war somewhere that threatened to wipe out an entire race of people, a tribe scattered and a prince with a destiny — *the first son of the first son.* This was bigger than the warren of rooms in the house. It was bigger than the backyard, which folded in on itself so tightly that from the roof it looked like a seashell surrounded with moss. What this man was describing was bigger even than this country made up of endless such yards along an endless ocean, with endless aunties and cousins and church services. Though my mother was in America somewhere and my father dead, this man reminded me that this place was temporary.

In fact, *all* places were temporary and so I had the power to float over it all.

Eventually, there were no more giggles or laughter. Even Cousin Violet seemed to pay attention. Cousin Mark stared intently at the floor, humbled, and Cousin Danny and Cousin Cecil were too defeated to feign indifference. The two Cousins June stared fearfully at my straightened back and expanded chest. In my mind, I was reciting the Oath of the Skull from *The Phantom*: "I swear to devote my life to the destruction of piracy, greed, cruelty, and injustice, in all their forms, and my sons and their sons shall follow me."

The shiny man was just the first. After him came a few more exiled ex-soldiers and itinerant Igbo patriots, all repeating variations of the same phrases. Not all of them shone with the same vigor; in fact, each seemed duller and increasingly less impressive. The spectacle soon wore off. The members of the family and other children from the neighborhood stopped coming to watch, and my visitor and I would be left alone in the parlor with Grandma and her dogs, all of them asleep. Some of these men left to find my mother, though I never heard from them again. This wasn't surprising because America was a place where people disappeared all the time, mothers in particular.

By the time I had completely lost the traces of our shared Nigerian accent, the men had stopped coming. And I was happy they did. They brought too much knowledge to assimilate about Biafra and Nigeria and my father and my godfather. Jamaica had its own complex expectations. I'd finally become indistinguishable from everyone around me, and I'd hoped that these men had realized that it was too late for my legacy. Perhaps America had been kind to them, and they lived there like my mother without regrets or legacies. Having learned to climb almost as well as Cousin Cecil and having learned how to survive Uncle Daddy's rages, I wanted those trees and that endless sky to do for me what they had done for everyone else on the island. I wanted them to help me forget all that came before it.

That kind of forgetting was difficult because in Jamaica Africa was everywhere. Images of the continent were painted on zinc fences, drums could be heard behind random bursts of foliage, and songs celebrating the continent blasted in the streets from the door-size speakers framing the entranceways of rum shops or from the stadium behind the house where reggae concerts were held during tourist season. We children had to hear those songs in the streets because such music was banned in the house and only the older girls would dare listen to it late at night when Big Auntie and Uncle Daddy were out. Africa was the promised land for itinerant Rastafarians who appeared on every corner or under every other tree. Something about that religion turned everyone into a preacher or prophet. They entranced many young people, including the older girls, because of their association with music or the fact that they were always in the news. But they terrified Big Auntie, who like most of her generation had grown up being told that those men with the snakes in their hair and the spider-webs in their beards kidnapped and ate children.

Like most people, my mother as a child in Jamaica had been taught that Africa was a source of shame. But she had then mi-grated to England only to fall in love with an African. Because I was so young, people still talked about it openly around me. In the 1950s and early 1960s, such a thing was beyond taboo — on both sides. Africans and Caribbean people thought themselves su-perior to one another, the former for having escaped chattel slav-ery and the latter for having escaped Africa. When folks back in Jamaica heard that my mother was going to marry someone from the continent, they were apoplectic. Africans were cannibals, even some close friends and members of her family said. She would be eaten upon arrival. Their men had many wives and she'd be locked in a harem somewhere and turned slave to her husband's pagan appetites. At the very least, she would disappear into that great void from which Jamaicans were lucky to have been deliv-ered in the first place by the light of Christ and the generosity of the Empire. Plus, she'd made it to England, the goal and destiny for all colonial subjects, so why would she ever leave?

I may have been too young to know the details of Nigeria, Gabon, and my father when my mother and I came to the island, but our arrival remained household lore. The way the adults told the story, my mother had carried me strapped to her back through fields of black smoke and across streets littered with the entrails of women and their children. It was as if she had come running across the ocean barefoot, back to the place where she was born. We had escaped, but from a place that many Jamaicans still associated with darkness, magic, and trauma. Despite the Africa-worshipping Rastafarians, "African" was still an insult, and being called that by Black people was the beginning of my consciousness of self.

Things only got worse after my mother left the island. The public knowledge that my mother was in America meant I was likely also to leave. That mobility was the ultimate sign of privilege and generated much resentment, especially among teachers who in those days were free to administer corporal punishment. It didn't take long, though, for me to begin to cherish my bruises and scars. Being beaten was like being punished for my African past and for my American future.

In a culture enamored with stories, the wilder and more colorful the better, I was able to exploit the continent, a place Jamaicans thought was the source of all stories. Through storytelling, I established some power in the household, in church, and at school. And I wasn't alone. We children were all desperate fantasists. We were made so by our hatred of our situation and our belief that we would soon be in America, England, or Canada, where we would quickly and joyfully forget the island and one another.

My particular skill at storytelling was due to the fact that I was a known reader who routinely risked a beating to read the books that Big Auntie kept on display in the parlor. Those books were for display alone, and for guests, but when night fell, I read them: *David Copperfield, Black Beauty, Treasure Island,* the tales of King Arthur. There was also *Robinson Crusoe, Kidnapped, Kim,* and others. Being caught with them under the sheets caused many of my beatings; worse were a couple of close calls when the candles I used for reading set fire to the sheets. These accidents never slowed down my hunger. I even traded with the Chinese boys at the end of the street whose family owned a shop that had books and comics with covers that had to be hidden from Big Auntie and Uncle Daddy due to their suggestion of paganism.

I learned in spite of my beatings that in Jamaica reading was publicly acknowledged as a good thing. I was encouraged in it as much by those who could read as by those who couldn't. Some of the latter would ask me to read to them, in the park, under the trees, on the roof. I even began teaching the house girls how to read when Sabbath ended and the house was gearing up for the new week. It wasn't unusual to walk through the streets and have some ragged Rastaman or khaki-clad sugar-cane cutter single me out as that boy "who good with book."

The actual amount of time I spent in that house before migrating to America remains contested. Where I exaggerated the length of time, my mother exaggerated its brevity. The truth was that I lived there for at least three years. The actual time was blurred by the fact that before my mother left for America I regularly stayed at the house after school and on Friday nights before church on Saturday. I would also spend holidays there. Also, Big Auntie never gave me my mother's letters after she left, so I had no choice but to accept that she hadn't written any. Making things worse, my rivals in the house told me again and again that my mother had forgotten me and would never send for me as was the case with so many other mothers who left their children to dissipate in the island sunlight.

Telling stories, then, was as much an act of survival as it was a display of faith. We spent hours doing so, usually in the tangle of iron, wood, and magic that was the backyard, or in the back of Uncle Daddy's bus when it was packed with the household and heading up into the country for trips that took entire days. And when we boys were alone, we clustered in the branches of the guinep and mango trees that hung over the wall separating our yard from the stadium. There we were safe from girls as well as the rude boys and young dreads who ringed the stadium and went through our pockets if they caught us on the grounds.

When we weren't focused on our histories or imagining our futures, we acted out American television programs, particularly the ones that featured Black Americans. This latter obsession drew into our competitions many of the beltless, shirtless, and shoeless boys from nearby yards. My cousins and I would even practice the accents we heard on those programs at church, thereby risking eternal damnation, which would be worth it if we could spend eternity sounding like Black Americans. Entire afternoons were spent at conferences held atop those trees, recalling our sources, debating modes of elocution like preachers of a faith we considered so orthodox that it did not need the indignity of a name.

None of us in the household were allowed to visit movie houses, which were where most of the learning of accents took place. They were also where all the rude boys and bad men congregated. The women there wore noisy bracelets on their ankles and had indifferent eyes. Rumor was that the oldest daughter in the family regularly went to movie houses. This was probably why she was the first to wear an Afro while the other daughters and cousins spent as much time ironing one another's hair as they did studying or praying. She spoke Black American almost as well as some of the actors on TV. She was the first to slap our palms when greeting us and the first to introduce us to foreign slang. After we'd gotten used to "giving her five" and listening to her speak what the house girls called "speaky-spokey," she began entangling us in handshakes we thought went on too long until we began seeing them on television and then in the streets.

She was the only one in the house who had any interest in my name. It was because of her that I always spoke it in full when asked and translated the middle part, Onuorah, which I knew meant "voice of the people." She especially loved that part. It seemed to guarantee an epic life or hearkened back to one shared before the white man came (and I'm sure she was the first person I heard use the phrase "the white man").

Thanks also to her I didn't shy away or pretend to be Jamaican when asked where I was from despite the mockery or ostracism that could follow. My willingness to publicly acknowledge my background impressed her. What mattered most to me was that she offered protection for very little in exchange. Along with Uncle Daddy, she was brutal when it came to meting out punishment to the children of the house. And when it came to people outside the house, she was fearless. She took on the boys in the street and even chased random Rastas out of the backyard who yelled "African bush baby" at me as they scrambled up the stadium wall.

The oldest daughter also protected me from her sisters and some of the older girls in the house in exchange for my stories. Calling them memories, I shared them with her while we crouched at the radio and record player in the parlor listening to reggae when Big Auntie and Uncle Daddy were away. Sometimes she would let me surf the static in between stations in hope of hearing a fragment of that song about Major Tom. Grandma would often be in the parlor with us amid her heavily breathing dogs, but her knowledge of what we were listening to was as limited as her hearing. In between reggae songs and with deepest gratitude, I joyfully crafted for my cousin an exquisite Africa she could use in the streets.

As entertaining and distracting as these stories could be, we children never lost sight of what they truly represented—our desire to leave the house and island. And that desire could be so strong that it created a distinct kind of madness among us, a delirium at times so strong that we became shameless. It eventually caused my stories to lose consistency and my lies to become at times so blatant and contradictory that I didn't care if they were believed or not or even if they were entertaining or not.

With others, the madness drove them to quite desperate acts. On each of their birthdays, the Cousins June religiously packed and repacked their suitcases, expecting to be taken to the airport to be finally reunited with their mother. Marching into the parlor, they wore their finest church clothes, held hands, and sat waiting until the sun appeared and disappeared. Cousin Robbie, who had been sent back to live with his grandparents in the countryside after learning his mother was not going to send for him, had gotten a young girl pregnant when we next heard of him. She was too young to carry the child to full term, and her "husband" buried it on the seashore next to a boat Robbie claimed to be building for the three of them. Eventually, he converted to Rastafari only to return to the house stabbed and lifeless just as the roots of his hair had begun knotting up and turning red from sea salt.

But for those who got visas, everything in the house, in the yard, on the island seemed to belong to them. At least for the days or weeks before their flights. Every word they said was true and their mood dictated the mood of house, school, and church. All prayers were for them. It was as if their skin in the glare of island sun had become indistinguishable from whiteness. When riding in Uncle Daddy's tour bus, they got to sit where tourists usually sat, and should they wish to skip worship service in the house —something otherwise unthinkable—all they needed to say was that they were packing. Big Auntie and Uncle Daddy would be excessively kind to them, affectionate even, knowing that the child who was leaving would now be responsible for their parent's continuing obligations to the household.

When my turn to leave the island finally came, I was robbed of that opportunity to move about the house with my nose upturned and my heart hard to the sudden warmth and affections of

the household. I wanted them to know that I had always understood that this condition was not permanent. I wanted them to
see how easy it would be to forget them. America would be my
revenge. I'd even prepared a speech, composed late at night with
the bedsheet over my head while my cousins who shared the bed
with me — Cecil and Danny — kicked at my chin and nibbled at
my ankles. It was the kind of speech one would expect from the
voice of the people. Because I didn't know I was leaving when
they rushed me to the airport, my speech was never heard. My departure seemed less a triumph than a mere accident, less a choice
than an act of deception.

We all expected that Cousin Violet would be the next to leave. She
was reaching the age where her unusual behavior and increasing
distance from the world we all shared was less and less explicable.
What had appeared magical or playful began to seem an advanc-
ing sickness to the older girls and outright demonic to the adults.
Big Auntie thought an early baptism would make a difference, but
when Cousin Violet came up from the green water cackling and
giggling, it seemed obvious that things would get worse.

She was silent all the way home from her baptism, sitting in
her usual seat in Uncle Daddy's Japanese bus, staring out the windows as wide as TV screens with her lips pursed tightly. Turns out

she'd kept some of the water in her mouth, and she spat it into an empty cola bottle as soon as we got home. She stopped it up with melted candle wax and toilet paper, and hid it somewhere in the backyard. She hid it so well that Cousin Mark exhausted himself trying to find it, as did Cousin Cecil. No matter how hard they hit her — knowing that her habit was never to make a sound, which made us boys ever more hostile due to envy — she never revealed its location.

Or maybe it would be Cousin Danny who would have been next to leave. We called him Architect due to his habit of drawing incredibly detailed maps and blueprints on the empty pages of school or church books or on pieces of cardboard. Sometimes he described his own buildings and cities as we lay in rapt attention in the trees or under the bed. His America was a visual one, and he proved to us that he belonged there by the vividness of his descriptions and the complexity of his cityscapes. The streets were precise and had angles so sharp that they seemed able to draw blood. The skylines were so balanced that the lack of trees or recognizable signs of nature was easily forgiven. Where I imagined a place with endless space, open and sprawling, Cousin Danny emphasized lines, walls, borders. If anyone had earned the right to leave simply by the amount of time spent waiting, it was Cousin Danny.

The only boy younger than I was Cousin Mark. We called him

Barrister because of his skill at argument and his composure when under pressure. He was beaten less than the rest of us and we attributed that to his gift for persuasion. The truth had more to do with the fact that his mother sent money directly to Big Auntie and Uncle Daddy, no barrels, no packages, just more cash than anyone else. Though his skills were lost on Big Auntie and Uncle Daddy — by the time things progressed to that level, there was never room for argument — Cousin Mark was able occasionally to mitigate the violence of the older girls against us. Because of his mother's money, we assumed he wouldn't be next. We thought him too valuable for the household to let go.

Cousin Cecil and I were the same age, but because of his particular ethnic mix, he looked younger or was allowed to act that way. Missionaries in particular loved him and commented on his almond eyes and curly hair, and kept him by their sides for as long as they stayed. He was the only boy who actually belonged in the house, so he would not be the next to leave.

It turned out to be me. I was the next to leave.

Returning home for lunch from school one day, I found the entire household arrayed as they had been when I met my first African. Since visits from Biafran ex-soldiers had long stopped, I didn't assume this to be a similar event. But everyone's eyes were on me as Cousin Cecil and I came in through the white metal gate that led through the bars surrounding the front patio. Most houses in that area had the same type of bars, all the same color white. It was as if everyone lived in birdcages.

Within seconds of our arriving, Big Auntie took from me a bag she'd asked me to carry to school, a pink floral-patterned shopping bag that my schoolmates had spent most of the morning mocking. It was a woman's bag, but I never dared ask her the reason why I had to take it. Cousin Cecil had laughed while my schoolmates called me "mamma-man" or "battyboy" as they followed me all the way to school that morning and back to the house that afternoon. It was obvious now that the bag was to guarantee that we'd be back home for lunch rather than roaming through the city streets with the children of "Sunday worshippers" as we were wont to do.

Big Auntie casually tossed the bag at Cousin Cecil. Then I was suddenly trying on new clothes, or rather new clothes were being tried on me. I was held fast by a couple of the older girls while at the same time a comb was doing its painful work. Big Auntie herself did the honors and in doing so conveyed the significance of this event. The clothes were truly new, not old and repackaged. They were better than the ones I wore to church and so crisp as to be uncomfortable against my skin. I had only one pair of good shoes, worn on Saturdays for service or at weddings, but apparently those weren't good enough so the household packed into the bus and rushed downtown to the shopping district. There they bruised my feet with shoes so tight and so fine that they had had to be brought out from the back of the store.

By the time I was swept back on the bus, some of the older girls surmised that I was going to be a page boy for one of the weddings the family regularly hosted for the church. Cousin Dale was the last to have received similar treatment, along with Cousin June the Younger who had been conscripted as the flower girl. They had both been called inside the house from the backyard, quickly dressed in clothes that had come from barrels that had been kept from them, and unceremoniously dragged to a wedding. The best part of that event was that, because it was their first wedding, the two of them actually thought that they too had gotten married. For almost a week they clung to each other and kept their distance from the tribes and factions in the house. They were eventually told the truth by the older girls, which saddened and angered the two children. We began calling Cousin Dale Divorcé.

They'd gotten "married" at Montego Bay's downtown Adventist church. Our regular church sat on the top of a hill with magnificent views of Montego Bay not only due to its altitude but also because it had no roof or completed walls. For as long as I could remember, it had been unfinished due to a never-ending need for donations and the erosion of support as younger parishioners migrated to the church downtown. We sat on stones during Sabbath school, and the preacher and choir sat on wooden planks stretched between unpolished bricks. The downtown church was where most of the weddings the family hosted were held. It had a roof, walls, colored glass, and a pool that allowed for indoor baptisms. Needless to say, the downtown church was preferred by the older girls. It was popular among the boys their age who were all too afraid of Big Auntie to visit the house except during the reggae shows when the crowds and the lights made the stadium's wall easy to climb without being seen.

But as the bus passed our hilltop church, there was nothing to explain what was happening. There hadn't even been a rumor from the house girls, who knew everything in advance of everyone and could be convinced to tell in exchange for anything from a spoon of condensed milk to a well-placed finger. Who was so important that we had to leave school at lunch and rush to buy shoes and trousers downtown?

We sat in our typical seats and played the usual games as the sea air blew brine through the bus windows. Through those windows came also the whine of the same old women selling fried fish or breadfruit with their faded head ties and skin cloudy with ash. There was the same sky, always blue even in storms, bluer even than the postcards that showed perfect waterfalls, which is what tourists said the moment they stepped out of the airplanes and into Uncle Daddy's tour bus. And there were the same tore-up-pants boys jumping on the running board to catch a ride whenever the bus slowed. We saw the same red-eyed Rastafari inspiring the same derision from Big Auntie but a snicker of complicity from the older girls, who seemed always to be plotting a coup that would never occur.

But then the bus turned onto the slender cliffside road that led to the airport. By the time the glare of landed planes was visible, the whispered debate had shifted. This mysterious trip had nothing to do with my being a page boy for a wedding. Someone was arriving. Cousin Danny suggested that it had to be my mother. I'd suspected as much but dared not assume anything for fear of being wrong. I didn't want what happened when Cousin Beverly got told one day that her mother was coming. She began behaving the way those about to leave were entitled to. Even after Big Auntie told her that her mother had canceled the trip, she sat in the parlor waiting in her church clothes, back straight and chin aimed at us aggressively. Why should she believe anyone in a house full of lies? She was there the next morning when we came out for worship service, which was held before sunlight made its way through the house.

If it was my mother who was arriving, that would explain the clothes and the shoes and the hair and the unexpected solicitude. Even if she was only visiting and would eventually become one of those mothers who merely sent down barrels and begged for annual photos of their children in church or school clothes, this trip would be a public victory. If this arrival was as close as I would ever get to my own departure, I would claim every moment, though not so obviously as Cousin Beverly did. I'd already learned from the boys in the streets, from American television, and from the Rastas that indifference was what real power looked like. A real man looked like he didn't care.

At the airport, Big Auntie dragged me from the bus. She pulled me through the crowd as if I were one of the many bags she carried to market. I lost my feet and glided across the tiles, fearful of being beaten if these new shoes were scuffed. My voice was impossible even for me to hear. There was no escape from the sound of Big Auntie's booming voice. Her hand clutched my wrist tightly, the same hand that I had once bitten deeply as she covered my mouth while I struggled against a tetanus injection after having my foot cut open while chasing the Two-Gun Kid into the backyard. That bite left a lifelong scar, my mouth permanently etched in her palm.

Despite my confusion, the chaos of the terminal was nothing new. For all of us children, the three institutions that governed our lives were school, church, and the airport. The last was the most sacred since its promises were most often fulfilled. But it was the first time any of us had entered the departure lounge. We'd usually be left outside peering in, checking for the faces of other children we knew. I looked back at my housemates to see if they understood the machinations behind this unexpected event, but all I could find in their faces was confusion and then jealousy. Had they known what was to happen to me, they would have become intimate. Some would have forgotten the scars and bruises they'd caused. They would have confessed past crimes or shared secrets as if I were a bottle to carry messages on an open sea. Others would have been uncommonly harsh, hoping to make it impossible for me to recall the past without wincing.

Because we were inseparable, Cousin Cecil was allowed to trail Big Auntie and me to and then beyond the departure lounge. With me on one arm, he still clutched that fateful plastic bag dotted with pink shapes and reddish textures. We'd both been in a growing panic since arriving at the airport. Cousin Cecil's cream-colored skin reddened about the ears and cheeks now that it became clear that this arrival was a departure. My mother was not coming; the Phantom was leaving. Cousin Cecil suddenly erupted in a gush of tears loud and clear enough to dwarf even Big Auntie's steady bellowing. His eyes became desperate as we approached the gate. He began to pull me, his loyal opposition, his brother in a world relentlessly of women, away from his own recently acquired mother. I enjoyed his bawling and the fact that his pulling slowed Big Auntie's progress through the crowd, causing her to bump into men who turned in anger only to curl up in front of her like certain weeds do when touched.

Held tightly behind his mother's geographic girth, Cousin Cecil still held the bag. He seemed unable to release it even after realizing its responsibility for the destruction of the world that we had made together. The last thing I registered before entering the plane was a line painted across the grainy tiles that was flanked by starched uniforms and defended by hardened expressions. It was the only thing with fresh paint in the entire airport. On one side in block letters was written PASSENGERS and on the other NATIVES.

I prayed for the plane to quickly break the terrestrial atmosphere like a spacecraft or to fold into itself like a time machine and open on the other side of held breath. There would be robots there and machines that didn't care where anyone came from and were eager to serve those of us lucky enough to arrive. That was where the song about Major Tom came from, I just knew it. But what soothed me most was imagining everyone calling out to me from the island below, begging me to come back as the ocean came crashing down on them. Jamaica was sinking like fabled Atlantis.

The flight attendants put small plastic wings on my lapel and touched my face. They had been waiting for me.

2

Heroes

These are the things I left behind.

• *My King James Bible,* left to me by my Jamaican grandmother. Her death soon after my mother had left for America brought my mother back to the island. It was a brief reunion, and though we spent some time together, my memory of her is filtered through a crowd of family and friends, her face behind a curtain of tears.

It was I who'd found my grandmother, or rather she who'd found me. I'd woken in the house she owned with my mother to find her sitting on the edge of my bed smiling broadly underneath her famously wide nose, muttering in the high-pitched voice that she usually reserved for screaming. Her wig was on, which was unusual for that early in the morning. She was gazing emptily at me, not as she would a stranger but as if I were someone else. By the time the house girl came running, my grandmother had made her way back to her room across the hallway. Her back was as straight as ever, reminding me as she died to always maintain my posture.

It was after this that I moved into Big Auntie and Uncle Daddy's house in Montego Bay. My grandmother's King James Bible was one of the few items that didn't need to be hidden from the other children. In it I kept my torn-out copy of the Oath of the Skull from *The Phantom* comic. I was too smart to keep it hidden in obvious places like the book of Psalms or Exodus or Revelations. I kept it where no one would look, in the narrow space between Zechariah and Malachi.

• *A yellow plastic star* from a toy cowboy set I'd stolen from Cousin Cecil. The word MARSHALL was still visible on it despite the badge having being mauled by the two house dogs that trailed Grandma. It was a visiting missionary from Loma Linda University who had

sent the gun set to Cousin Cecil for Christmas. It arrived complete
with a bandolier, a star, a thin rubber mask, and a plastic gun, and
it immediately conferred on cousin Cecil the title of Two-Gun
Kid despite the fact that the gun was confiscated by Uncle Daddy,
who deemed it inappropriate for Seventh-day Adventists.

I should have stolen the mask instead.

• *Three of Cousin Danny's sketches of buildings* taken in retaliation
for the theft of one of my books that was eventually found without its cover. Danny denied stealing it, but the empty white back
was scribbled with the dimensions of some unfinished streetscape
with a horizon full of skyscrapers. Even though Cousin Danny
had started this back-and-forth, he still gave me a vicious beating
on an afternoon memorable because of the winds announcing a
storm.

Storms or hurricanes meant no school. With the electricity
gone, each of the tribes or nations in the house huddled in its own
zone. Storms made the backyard even more wondrous as water
flooded Montego Bay and we launched armadas of paper boats
from the back door. If it was a proper hurricane, we would be sent
into the hills above the city to stay with aunts and uncles older
than Grandma and who needed to be reminded who we were each

time. There we waited for the rains and winds to stop so we could tramp through acres of mud deep enough to sink down to the belly and go hunting for blue crabs washed up by swollen rivers and deposited in unlikely places such as latrines in hilltop villages. As we opened the doors, the crabs spilled out in the hundreds, crackling and skittering blue.

That afternoon I'd run from cousin Danny out into a wind so strong that it slowed me down enough for him to catch me in the empty green lot at the end of the street where the circus would be in those summers when there was no revival tent service held there. Now the lot held people from the hills outside Montego Bay who had lost their homes in the latest storm. They had built fires in empty oil drums and made beds out of thickets of weeds and brush. The smell of burned corn was everywhere. The sight of these people and their sudden shantytown slowed Cousin Danny to a stop.

Realizing I was running without being chased, I turned back to see him fall to one knee, his fingers circled like a lens. It was a position he'd learned watching surveyors when they came to examine our roofless and incomplete church. Watching the refugees scuffle and wander, hearing the children and mothers call to one another over the zinc and cardboard used to make walls and roofs, cousin Danny forgot all about me. He was there to the rescue, saving the people, building a city, delivering them however briefly into shelter.

• *My church clothes left in Grandma's closet*. High-altitude shoes with thick wooden heels, pants thin at the waist with wide thighs and flared at the cuffs that still looked good even though the cuffs were closer to my calves than my ankles. This was high fashion then. My four-pocket dark gray bush jacket with thick black stitching around all the pockets was folded on top of the same hanger that held the pants. There is a picture somewhere. I was quite sure I looked just like a member of the Jackson Five or other Black American groups whose pictures were all over the girls'-room walls.

In the left top pocket of the bush jacket was a small empty packet of sugar Cousin Cecil and I had taken from one of the hotels where Uncle Daddy collected tourists for day trips. We spent the entire evening and night expecting to be found out and beaten. We made sure not to share what we'd done with any of the other children, even Cousin Mark or Cousin Danny, for fear of the power they would then have over us. That we weren't caught gave the sugar an additional sweetness.

The next day in the schoolyard, the boys from our class stood in a queue that disappeared into the distance as I remember it. They came forward with one finger extended humbly for a taste of authentic American sugar. Cousin Cecil complained that we should be charging them and said that we could even have mixed in regular Jamaican sugar to keep this concession alive. I refused. I'd learned from America that power worked best through flagrant acts of generosity.

• *My "foolish space books,"* as Big Auntie called them, left in Hortense's room at the back of the house. Hortense didn't think them ungodly as did everyone at church and didn't raise a fuss whenever she saw the covers. For her, they were not satanic at all. They were about the many places other than heaven or hell. I wondered what my mother would think of them. Word in the house was that she wasn't *truly* a Seventh-day Adventist and only passed as one in order to attend their college, considered by many to be the best on the island.

• *A 45 record.* The label was so scratched on one side that the name of the singer or group was unreadable while the opposite was marked VERSION with a simple drawing of a lion's head. Church Brother Wesley's youngest boy found it in the bushes on the far side of the stadium where it no doubt had fallen out of the record box of some local sound system. Knowing its value and risk, he had run straight across the park with it clutched to his chest. Any boy from any household or from any of the schools in that narrow corner of Montego Bay would have done anything to get that treasure. He arrived at our house too terrified by his transgression to keep it.

Like all of us, he'd never touched a record before and imagined it too fragile to be put into his schoolbag. As he'd approached our front gate with his frightening prize, a boy named Garth had edged up to the wall that separated his yard from ours. Garth had been identified as an up-and-comer by the local rude boys who lurked around the gates of the stadium behind our houses. They did him the honor of nodding their heads when they saw him walking through the streets with his pants open wide enough to billow at each step. He was the first of his age to wear that street style, zipper and belt buckle left open, and he chewed a long stem of grass in what we called cowboy fashion. He leaped up now to the top of the wall, eyeing whatever it was that was so closely clutched, suspecting its value by the desperate attempt to conceal it.

We were at the base of the guinep tree playing cricket with a bat made from broken fence wood and a ball shaped by wrapping tightly what cousin Cecil claimed were miles and miles of wire. We heard the house girls screaming at Brother Wesley's boy to stop running like that in the house. Breathless, he stopped in front of his older brother, who was playing cricket with us, and handed the record to him before resting his hands on his knees so he could breathe. Seeing what he held, we immediately looked up to the tree-lined high wall that separated all of the yards from the stadium. As expected, Garth was already there with some picky-head boy whose penis could be seen dangling from his open pants as he stepped across overarching tree branches. Before they had a chance to climb down the wall, we went inside the house, gathering in the washroom among the damp clothes hanging from wires stretched from corner to corner.

After a restorative silence, the boy, terrified, said he wanted us to keep the record. We *had* to keep it.

Cousin Cecil reminded the brothers that reggae music was not allowed in our house. The record would also be dangerous to keep because for some members of the church its very shape and the wide hole inside would be so suggestive of its sound that it would be blasphemous even as an object. The only records allowed in the house were American country music and gospel, all of which came full-size with small holes and were clearly labeled with pictures of white people and endless sky.

Terrified by the possibilities of response to this obscene item, my cousins offered no resistance to my claiming primary ownership of the record along with sole responsibility should it ever be found. I was, after all, not quite one of them. I was from Africa, so salvation was always a question. My agreeing to keep it was also an acknowledgment that it would be hidden so well that there would be no evidence of it should any of these boys decide to use it against me. Hiding this object was an act of greater value than the crude act of listening to it. Centuries in the future, this object would be the final evidence that the island or its language or its people ever existed. But I'd make sure no one found it even then.

• *One of my father's medals.* It was a Biafra Air Force pin caked with dirt but not chipped or broken, the clasp miraculously still working. I found it while walking one evening through the long hallway that connected the front of the house to the central kitchen and then opened out to the maze of rooms in the back where Hortense and the other house girls slept. Beyond that was the washing room and then the yard, which spilled over into as many other yards as spilled into it.

I'd noticed the medal's muted glimmer in a pile of dirt left behind by someone who was sweeping just as Sabbath fell and knew to leave the job unfinished so as to not incur the wrath of Big Auntie for whom the moment of sunset was absolute. Strangely enough, I knew immediately what it was. It had been kept in a storage room that my mother had left in Big Auntie's care. How long had it been mingled with the dirt and refuse of this house?

• *A small American flag* wrapped tightly around itself and shoved inside a long, thin enamel pipe, the kind that Uncle Daddy used or sold for building or plumbing. It was mounted on a black pencil-thin pole with its once gold spear-shaped head chipped and dulled. The flag was safe inside the pipe because it was buried beneath many other pipes on the side of the house that was too dense with brush and zinc panels to permit trespass.

The flag had been given to me by one of a set of twin cousins from America who visited one summer, my first Black Americans though they were originally from Jamaica. They were from a previous generation of children, having migrated to America years before any of us had arrived in the house and before Cousin Cecil had been adopted. Upon arriving, they displaced Cousin Cecil and me from our bed except for late nights when one of them would bring either Cousin Cecil or me into bed while his brother slept or read comic books by candlelight. There he gave us sweets and chocolates that we couldn't get in Jamaica while feverishly rubbing his hands between our legs and his stiffened groin against ours until in a shudder he pushed us back on the floor. Whoever had been in bed with him would share the sweets and chocolates with the others, even smaller cousins who thought it unfair that they were not allowed to earn them on their own.

Big Auntie nicknamed the cousins Dilly and Dally. We worshipped them as if they were stars from television or heroes from movies we heard about but could not watch. They arrived complete with the accent, clothes, and an impatience that seemed cultivated and therefore easily imitable. Cousin Cecil and I traveled with them to visit their grandparents up in the countryside near Reading. They refused to use the outhouses, and as far as we could see, they never did.

One afternoon the cousins sent me, Cousin Cecil, and a herd of local country boys to catch as many bush rats as we could find. The two cousins walked behind us wearing actual blue jeans and tennis shoes. They carried a small wooden cage they had made. We eventually caught two fat mangy things with teeth as long as the nails on their feet and a smell that made even the country boys turn up their noses. The cousins had us put them in the cage before leading us back toward the house. We put the cage on a tree stump and delighted in watching the two beasts crawl over and around each other, pushing their filthy snouts in between the crooked wooden bars.

The cousins insisted we gather as much brush and dried grass as possible, which was easy since it was high summer. The grass and leaves felt like strips of paper or Grandma's white hair. Then they banished the local boys, pushing and slapping them violently away. One of the cousins went to make sure there were no adults around their grandparents' yard and sent Cousin Cecil and me to check the kitchen and the front garden. We felt a sudden and overwhelming excitement, much like the feeling we got when someone was arriving at the airport or when the one American cousin was deciding which of us would briefly share his bed.

We piled the brush and grass around the cage, and put a heavy piece of wood on the top. Despite our preparation, we were surprised when the cousins lit the brush and leaves. Cousin Cecil and I stared at each other briefly, suddenly unable to communicate even silently as we usually could. It was much easier than we thought to watch the cage quickly envelop in flames. First the bush rats squirmed around and under each other, then pushed harder against the bars. Then they too went up in a flash, and their natural stink and the added stink of burning fur and flesh blended with the smoke.

Faster than I would have imagined, the rats stopped pushing and squirming, and just sat quietly. Their eyes trained past us at the local boys who had slowly begun returning from the bushes, fences, and corners. The cousins from America didn't shoo them away this time, transfixed as they were by the eyes of the rats that began to grow and expand until there was no doubt that they could see all of us. The rats watched us watching them, and we watched until those eyes burst with a sound like an echoed rhythm, bubble gum popping, or Ping-Pong balls suspended by skillful players.

The cousins slapped each other's palms and did that intricate handshake that we'd learned from Big Auntie and Uncle Daddy's oldest daughter. Then they smiled with great satisfaction and let out deep breaths.

• *The few remaining plastic soldiers* from a set I'd liberated from the top of Big Auntie's dresser where she kept some of the toys and books sent by my mother. I didn't share them with any of the others even after many of the soldiers became unrecognizable from being chewed by the house dogs into mere lumps of green plastic. With them, I restaged that war that had been the cause of our arrival on the island. I rebuilt a country, though, without women since there weren't any in the set. There was no need for refugees or immigrants in this country because our side always won. With these toys, we could be heroes in a world made exclusively of fathers.

3

Life on Mars

My mother thought that when I kicked her during the night it was because I was still wrestling with my cousins back in Montego Bay. Sometimes it did begin that way as I moved away from her grasping fingers or heard her dream-talking about bombed-out villages, hollowed-out bodies, and children shaped like spiders. But ultimately it had nothing to do with Cousins Cecil or Danny or Mark. On this small bed that magically folded into a couch in the daytime, I was punishing her for leaving me on that island.

It started at the airport immediately after landing and my having been escorted out of the plane by the flight attendants. My mother approached while I was scanning the ceilings and high corners for the source of the robot voices announcing arrivals and departures. She was thinner than I remembered and visibly shaken in the bleaching lights. My grandmother's flaring nose was the first thing I recognized on her face. I turned toward her, imagining the purple mask of the Phantom on my face, and raised myself to full height. My mother retaliated by falling to her knees. We were face-to-face. She'd achieved the same sweatless scent that tourists and missionaries had. Like babies, the house girls said, Americans smelled like babies. They took too many baths and drank too much milk. I looked at the passengers crisscrossing the tiles, embarrassed that they might think me a newcomer when my mother was the real foreigner.

The group of women who came with her encircled us as she held my arms up above my head and turned me around to read my skin. She felt my neck, ribs, belly, and shoulders, and lifted my shirt. She traced her fingers down the middle of my back, and when she pushed too hard at a scar, I shivered at the sweetness of her discovery. She made a sharp intake of breath as she discovered each scar and bruise. She prodded and touched, and I winced and gasped. We would communicate this way for days.

My disappointment grew when I saw the women with her. I'd expected men in America. I'd earned them. Instead, there were just more aunties, Cousin Danny's mother and the mothers of both Cousins June. There were others, but their names were unimportant. Aunties were the same everywhere and were apparently everywhere. They were waiting for me to look up at them. They wanted forgiveness or some temporary form of it that could last until their own child arrived. On behalf of my peers left back on the island, I denied them even as they collapsed around me competing for an inch of unbruised skin.

My mother wasn't wearing dark glasses as she did in every photograph I could recall. The ones I remembered best were where she looked like a film star, the "Jackie O of Biafra," I'd heard say, though it would be years before I knew who Jackie O was. Here in the airport, she seemed too simple to be what the stories and the photos said of her. Was she wearing a wig? That was enough to make me doubt everything, even the story of my birth and maybe also the war.

The women shook their heads and made sounds of disbelief and surprise. It was as if they had just left Saturday service but were still clustered near the church entrance. The fact that they had no shame embarrassed me deeply. I was grateful I couldn't see beyond them to the citizens and passengers no doubt frowning at this spectacle.

"Look how him so hungry," one said, the hands of another on

my shoulder tightening the grip of yet another on my arm. "Look how him so slight and skinny and soon turn close to nothing."

"Jesus Lord, how them treat we *pickney* them so?"

"Him look sick like African baby for true, like him have kwashi—"

My mother shot a look at this auntie that silenced her and the others shook their heads. After a beat, they began again.

"At least him come, at least him arrive safe and fine in him new shoes and clothes, God bless."

"Yes, Lord . . . God bless."

A collective moan, an ululating sigh, then the hydra-headed beast reached its multiple arms towards the ceiling. My mother closed her eyes as if she was praying. She was praying. They all were. I thought about Cousin Violet's baptism and wondered where she had hidden that bottle.

Anyway, I was in America.

Soon that was yesterday, then the day before. Then it was a week ago and last month. Sometimes, mercifully, it never was, especially when the weather started to go colder than I'd ever known. The boy with the bruises on his back had proven an entire island wrong. He was now in a place where electricity never faltered, water ran hot and cold, and television never ended. He had a new transistor radio, his very own pillow, and a mother who blamed herself for his bruises. A child couldn't ask for more.

Because I had arrived at my mother's apartment in Washington, DC, at night and she went to work every evening and most days, those first weeks were like an extended twilight. The room was kept dark, shades drawn. I remember the intense vertigo that came from looking out of them. I don't recall what floor we were on, but we were higher than any building I'd ever seen on the island. I wasn't to open the shades or answer the phone unless it rang once then stopped, rang twice then stopped, and then I would know it was her. I remember only sleeping and waking and keeping myself awake. To fall asleep was to risk returning to Grandma's room in the bed I shared with my cousins, and to the breathing of the dogs and the smell of Grandma's bedpan. I still anticipated the call to morning worship.

The apartment was so filled that it felt much smaller than it was. There were unpacked boxes, suitcases, and paper and plastic bags stuffed with paper and plastic bags. In corners were boxes filled with plastic bottles and bottle tops, pencils and pens, empty pill containers, and unopened goods marked with the names of the various hospitals in this city where my mother had worked. Most of our bowls, cups, and saucers were from those hospitals, labeled as such or with the names of drugs being promoted. Bags of clothes choked the bedroom closet and shoeboxes were stacked against the walls. Inside those shoeboxes were rarely shoes, but medical supplies and first aid kits, syringes, cotton, and gauze. There were books too—first aid manuals, Bibles, and those for learning English. Colorful African fabrics made the floor of the closet inches higher than it should have been. Western clothes hung from wall hooks, many still with price tags and wrapping. New brooms and mops were tied in tight bundles leaning against doorjambs. Under the main apartment window like a safety barrier were more books, magazines, and stacks of blank paper wrapped in tight plastic.

There were no proper plates in the kitchen. The ones we used were made of paper. There were no true knives and forks either. We used plastic. These were not thrown away after being used. My mother washed, saved, and collected them until the drawers were so filled that they sometimes couldn't be closed completely. Even the paper plates were wiped clean unless they were too damp from the food. Realizing how easy it was for them to be ruined, she made sure we stacked two or three together when we used them.

There were boxes of pictures and letters, some obviously unsent since they were written by my mother and addressed to people whose names I also saw on the backs of photographs. Some of the photographs were from Nigeria and Gabon and a great many from Biafra—the kwashiorkor children, mostly, heads and bellies swollen from malnutrition. Later I learned that the British-backed Nigerian government had blockaded our small country during that four-year war. Just as food and medicine were kept out, communication—and evidence of genocide—was kept in. Falling from the boxes too were fragments of letters, notes, and bits of paper scribbled with dates and cryptic phrases like *The British didn't stop it because it was all for oil!* Or *This is not our country* or *People can only really hurt what they see* or handwritten lines of poetry. One was "I was the sole witness to my own homecoming," written by a poet named Chris Okigbo.

Under the couch were boxes so packed that one had only to reach in and scoop photos of her and other nurses in uniform, of my grandmother in the small town where we lived before Montego Bay, of train stations and brick hospitals in England, and of her life in Nigeria before and during the war. The photographs were all mixed up, 1940s Jamaica, early 1950s London, Nigeria in the 1960s, Gabon and Jamaica in the 1970s—the only thing that held them all together were the images of starving children, layers of newspaper clippings about the war, documents marked from the state of Biafra, faded letterhead with official signatures, bank notes, and stamps. As the country became more isolated, the formalities of statecraft seemed to have increased. This was the archive of a country too hastily erected and too quickly destroyed to have established an official history. Its golden age was measured in moments.

In lieu of science fiction, fantasy, or history, this was all I had to feed my voracious appetite for reading. These boxes were where my new education began.

There were magazine articles about how Americans and Europeans had responded to the war. The Operation Airlift Biafra Benefit in New York featured rock stars such as Jimi Hendrix and Joan Baez. These names meant nothing to me then. Apparently, John Lennon of the Beatles—one of my father's favorite groups—had refused an award from the Queen partly due to England's support for the Nigerian Federal Government. There was news about a white woman in Paris who burned herself to death in front of the Nigerian embassy in protest against the violence against the Igbo people. A young American student at Columbia University also immolated himself with a sign on his body that read STOP GENOCIDE, SAVE NINE MILLION BIAFRANS. The most notorious reaction to Biafra's international impact was US President Lyndon Johnson's demanding his State Department "get those damned nigger babies off my TV set!"

One image in particular comes to mind. With it, Biafra ceased to be family myth or folktale. It may have been a single scene, but there were at least three photos of it—a cleanly decapitated man wearing only trousers and sprawled on a table, his head nowhere to be seen. One photo was a close-up of the severed neck. The others focused on separate cuts all over his body but never strayed too far from that primary absence.

There were random words written on bits of paper or the backs of envelopes. My mother had the habit of subscribing to "word of the month" clubs and bought calendars that featured vocabulary. There were Igbo words, Yoruba, French, but also pidgin. Some were obviously new to her as she moved from country to country. Some were archaic. I remember one in particular, *calentura,* which was written on the back of a picture of a large ship of the sort she must have taken to England in the 1950s. Not knowing its meaning made the image of the ship more memorable, and I began imagining that the word suggested what it must be like to feel the rolling of water beneath one's feet.

Gaining some sense of her history from this archive, however, didn't weaken my resolve to punish her. I was barely ten years old and my Jamaican scars still too fresh. If not to signal some softening of my feelings but perhaps to make myself useful, I attempted to throw things away. Maybe an emptier room would make it easier to keep one's distance. I tossed away empty bottles and jars, unused drinking straws and stacks of paper napkins and broken pens that poured from under the bathroom sink if the doors opened too quickly. Maybe all this stuff made sense in Africa or Jamaica where all objects were valuable, but in my view, she'd completely missed the point of America.

I didn't think she'd be able to track what remained and what was gone, but she seemed wounded by the absence of each and every thing no matter how small. There were moments of panic, one particularly acute when she began looking for a small wooden egg, notched and scarred. I thought it was simply a child's toy, perhaps mine. I was shocked at the depth of her hurt over the idea that I might have tossed out the egg and by her attachment to, essentially, rubbish. She told me she was saving everything in the apartment to send to Jamaica and Nigeria when she could afford to and that we should never waste things because you never know when *anything* could save your life. She'd lost everything too many times to lose anything again. Even an embittered ten-year-old could understand that.

She never did send any of these items back to Jamaica or Nigeria, but she continued planning to do so. That was her primary psychological setting. It was a way of not fully accepting our arrival. I assumed it was a trait of women because my aunties were always trying to convince themselves that they could and would leave this country anytime they wanted. It was as if it was necessary to remind themselves that they'd chosen to come here and that they could take it or leave it. The country had no power over them.

I came to realize that she did understand the point of America, so well that she had been rebelling against it long before I'd arrived. She'd landed in a place where things seemed to evaporate or were too easily replaced. These mundane and banal items, stacked as they were, layered and dense with accretion, represented a stand against loss.

Upstairs from us lived a nun who had known us during the war. Aunt Ngozi had been my nanny at some point in Gabon and smelled like mothballs. This made sense after I discovered that she kept her clothes in a travel trunk despite having lived in the same apartment for years before my mother's arrival. I have no recollection of her ever being outside the building. She never used the elevator and always arrived at our door sweating, her sheen emphasizing the pristine darkness of her skin.

Aunt Ngozi was the second person to call me *the first son of the first son*. For the first few weeks, she visited our cramped and tiny apartment simply to stare at me, rocking back and forth on the edge of a couch that at nightfall miraculously transformed into the bed that my mother and I shared. Aunt Ngozi was never able to look at me, talk to me, or touch me without reminding me that my father was a hero to the Igbo people and that she'd cried *forever* when she heard that he had been killed and thought that we had been killed also only to learn that we were only for a time lost somewhere in the bush where the children were swollen with kwashiorkor and rivers overflowed with chopped and bloated bodies.

Fortunately, she only spoke in outbursts. Her creaky voice exploded in all directions but only for concentrated moments of time. With spit froth speckling her lips, words left tracks across her chin. Then she would retreat, arms folded, head bowed, eyes staring so intently that I could feel them on my skin like ants.

She took it upon herself to begin teaching me Igbo.

"*Nno,*" she said whenever she saw me, which meant "welcome." "*Nno,*" with her mothball scented hands holding my face. "*Nno.*"

"Say *d'aalu,*" said my mother. "*D'aalu.*"

But this was America. I thought there were more important things to learn.

Eventually, I was allowed to leave the apartment on my own and walk upstairs to stay with Aunt Ngozi whenever my mother was going to be home later than usual or on rare nights when she had an overnight shift. Aunt Ngozi didn't have a television or even a radio and her apartment was smaller than ours. To not have a television in a country where broadcasting was permanent and channels were multiple was unforgivable. I never brought my transistor radio because Aunt Ngozi didn't understand my ongoing search for that song about Major Tom, and the one time I brought it, the static rattled her. She wasn't able to speak until the radio was off and then rubbed her skin as if the white noise was creeping across her body.

Her windows were always closed, covered with dark curtains, and the heat sweltering. The apartment smelled of old, wet paper, and I imagined dark corners mossy green and fetid with life. Though largely empty of furniture, the apartment also had one of those miraculous extending couches and a small table in the kitchen covered with photographs and letters. While my mother kept multiple items, Aunt Ngozi kept only paper. Beneath the table was a box of passport photos of dozens of African priests and nuns and missionaries, most of them dressed in white. I don't remember there being anything on her walls, no crosses, no pictures of a crucified Christ or the Virgin Mary, and no images of the countryside churches or frolicking sheep typical in Jamaica. She had no bookshelves, which made sense because she hadn't any books at all.

Sometimes I awoke to find her rooting through the box of passport photos or the photo albums. I would catch her making the sign of the cross on her chest and shaking her hands as if to rid them of something sticking to them. And sometimes when airplanes passed too loudly by, she ducked against the corner of the windows.

Without a television, a radio, or books, I spent my time with her looking at photographs or listening to her stories about the war, about the bombs that razed villages and the hordes of Igbo people scattering east and south knowing that to go west toward Lagos was to face indifference and to go north was to face death, and in its wake, your body would be defiled. It was in the North that the violence had started, as the Muslim Hausa people turned on the Christian Igbos who had lived among them for so long. There had been a coup in the South, or perhaps two of them, led by Igbo soldiers, which triggered the paranoia of the Muslims. The Hausas responded by attempting to cleanse the newly formed nation of Igbos, who then began retreating to their ancestral lands in the East, which is where the nation of Biafra was soon declared in response. It didn't help that Biafra sat on one of the largest oil deposits discovered on the African continent. According to my mother, this was something that my godfather—who made the declaration—thought a source of power.

Aunt Ngozi had seen many people burned alive as they fled to the East, left smoldering in dirt roads as warnings to other road-weary refugees. The violence a message of a power so great that it could reduce human life to mere signs. That is how she knew God had chosen the Igbos to suffer for the sins of the entire continent and that he had intended for that suffering to be public.

The headless man made some sense now, like a symbol or fragment of speech.

"This is why it is true for everybody to be calling Igbo people the Jews of Africa. Do you know about these things? Has your mother told you about these things? Do you even know that she had to kidnap you from your own people to save you?"

My mother wouldn't start telling me anything until I was impervious to her discomfort. Aunt Ngozi insisted on telling me despite its being against my will. The telling was harsh, her spittle and her penchant for emphasizing brutality too much even though I was at the age when I was consistently testing my ability to sustain unpleasant things. Many of these stories ended in my being clutched to Aunt Ngozi's musky bosom as she prayed and slept. In those weeks before I could go down to the lobby by myself and before I started school, she turned the two apartments into something akin to that refugee camp in Gabon where she said we'd been reunited with her and then other friends.

"Governments would not help us then, only charities and churches, and many of those people died as well, shot down in planes or just killed."

There were photographs of airlifts and bomb casings and bullets littering the ground like peanut shells.

"Those boys," she said, pointing at half-naked youths bent over in the dust against the wide-leaved greenery of Eastern Nigeria. "Their job was to find bullets and take them from dead men and give them to the living ones. They were there also making weapons. Your father's greatness came from being the commander of the Biafra Air Force with no planes at first and no pilots, just Igbo people learning how to do these things and some madmen from Europe called mercenaries and some who believed in your godfather even though they were white men. He was a hero to white men too."

She remembered the shock that ran through the camp in Gabon when it was discovered that a foreign woman had arrived on an airlift with a baby boy strapped to her back like a native woman. This woman wasn't Igbo or even African.

"No matter what they tell you when you go back there," she once said before sleeping, "your mother was a hero to take you from that family after your father was killed by that shrapnel that was everywhere in those times."

There were no details about my father's death in my mother's boxes, drawers, and bags and piles of paper.

"No matter how much they blame her and call her kidnapper, your mother is a hero. Should she have stayed behind? And left you in that place? No, no, God, no. Your mother was a better African than them because she wanted to be one whereas they could only be what they were. Only a hero can become someone else. And that baby boy was you, *the first son of the first son*. God can do great things. There are times when he shows you that he can. But then sometimes he will show you that he won't."

Aunt Ngozi's faith had stretched enough to suit my own nascent thinking about the universe. During the worst of the war, she'd begun to wonder if the suffering of the Igbos and the mad-eyed violence of the Northerners were proof that there was no God. She'd always assumed their gods were ultimately the same but for the difference in name and mode of worship. For Allah to sanction or require this violence only fed the suspicion that there could be no God at all, Muslim or Christian. But the war had confirmed that God did exist, just not in the way she had taken for granted. Kwashiorkor and the violence had taught her that perhaps he was just not a god to be worshipped. Instead, he was to be feared for an indifference that in the face of all this chaos and suffering made him divine. After all, only a god could ignore what she saw. Only God could allow it.

She added, "The Yoruba believe creation came from a drunk god. We don't have the benefit of such explanation."

There were pictures among my mother's papers of children who had been hungry for so long that they no longer knew how to eat. They seemed as if they were actually posing for the camera, with food from American aid tins clotting their faces. Even the flies seemed picturesque, posed. These children looked like stranded outer space travelers. To see them as belonging to this world made it harder to look at them.

Aunt Ngozi's particular vision of God was the first to take hold of me in the wake of my time in Jamaica, those years of Seventh-day Adventist fire and brimstone. I'd thought that there were two options, God or godlessness. But this notion of an *indifferent* God was as powerful an idea as any I'd heard or read about. It might have come from Aunt Ngozi, but I cherished it as my first great American notion. ·

This was a god of indifference but also of forgetting. Better yet a machine, one too complex to acknowledge its smaller parts or recall its processes and effects. This machine would have to be all-knowing and therefore know its own limits so it could choose to erase portions of its memory. That will to erase was an act of love because it came from a desire to find us again but as if new and strange and therefore redeemable.

4

Suffragette City

S till, the absence of men troubled me. Weeks and months
in America and this remained a city, a country perhaps, of
women. Aunties upon aunties. I began to wonder if only women
and children were immigrants. And were the only men here
white? That's all I saw in and around the gleaming glass-and-
metal spaceship that was our building. And what happened when
boys became men? Did they remain immigrants?

I came here expecting not only to become an American but
specifically a Black American. But there were no Black Americans
anywhere, at least none I can remember, until my mother began

taking me through the city. Even then it was clear that there was a barrier between us and them despite the similarity of skin. It was never discussed, but it was rigidly maintained and wouldn't be explained until I started school.

Some aunties visited the apartment in those first weeks and months, but it was some time before I began to see them and their children regularly. Even after earning my right to stray from the path between our apartment and Aunt Ngozi's, I spent almost all of my time in the apartment complex. There were days I'd meet my mother downstairs as she came home and ride the elevator up with her. The joy of this freedom would translate into moments of warmth she was happy to receive.

But then, amid a swirl of new cousins, aunties, and the familiar ache of absent men, life in America began to resemble life in Jamaica. The aunties were most often nurses like my mother. Along with an entire generation of Caribbean people, they'd gone after World War II to rebuild the "Mother Country" — they still called it that without irony. Regardless of how they'd been treated upon arrival in England, they felt they had rescued an empire they still felt a part of. It was England that had needed them, reached out for them. In saving it, they were superior to it and therefore to the racism they encountered. Due to their skills, some eventually made their way to the United States and Canada even if it meant leaving their children in Jamaica.

Many of the women she knew from nursing school in England. This world of immigrant nurses and their families would lead to a strange mix of loneliness and community that characterized my childhood—endless aunties and a relentless flow of new cousins. We quickly assembled networks of family, but our time together was often short. This may have made us value those quick intimacies, but it made us also quick to detach since we were already prepared for connection to end.

One of my new aunts in DC, whom I remember only as Tante, was from Gabon. She and her children became my new family along with an aunt from the Caribbean named Carmen and her children. Aunt Carmen had known my mother in London and had lost track of her after she'd been swept off her feet by my father and hurried to Nigeria. Aunt Carmen remembered that time well because she, like many of the others, had thought my mother was making a terrible mistake. She'd thought her dead when she heard about the Nigerian Civil War—what would a Jamaican woman do in that madness?

Tante had four children. Her oldest son's French name was Hans. He was older than I by a year or two. There were two girls, one whose French name was Geneviève and who was exactly my age. The other was younger, but I don't remember her name. The only one not born in Gabon was a baby always swaddled in native cloths. The family had a house girl who spoke only their native language and a few words in French. A house girl was something none of us had anymore, so this seemed both an incredible extravagance and a sign of what we had all lost. In Africa house girls and house boys were such an intrinsic part of life that to arrive in a country where they were available only to the wealthy was a shock even children could feel. Tante's family also had a house, which placed them at the very top of our small social world.

Big Auntie and Uncle Daddy's daughters had claimed that when my mother and I landed in Jamaica my first words to them were in French. "*Bonbon*," I supposedly had said, which to their ears sounded like the Jamaican profanity *bumbo*. They'd initially assumed them native African words, which no doubt confirmed whatever ideas they'd had about Africa. They disbelieved my mother who angrily told them that the words were French and that Africans spoke English, French, and other "civilized" languages. France had been one of the few countries to support Biafra, albeit secretly, with weapons, mercenaries, food, and medicine.

But Tante was not as sympathetic to the French people as my mother was. She thought them no different from the British. They had colonized Gabon, after all, and were also after the oil discovered in Igboland before the war. In her view the British hoped to get it by supporting the federal government, the French hoped to have privileged access if they sided with Biafra. It was

Tante's family we'd stayed with once we left the refugee camps
—or were rescued from them, said Aunt Ngozi, eyes wide and
glazed as we relived each and every moment in the grotto of her
apartment. I was thankful to be seeing less and less of that room as
I began to spend time with the new aunties and cousins.

Tante's husband was a diplomat who had traveled between Gabon, Paris, Nigeria, and the Ivory Coast. They spoke of him often and displayed photos of him in every room of their spacious
home. He'd been placed under house arrest in Gabon. But then all
word from or about him stopped. Uncle had been gone so long
that his presence was felt largely through a pause in the family's
language, a linguistic instability as they struggled to determine
which tense to use when speaking of him. I remember Tante saying to my mother that for us it was easy. At least we knew that my
father was actually dead.

Aunt Carmen's children were named Karina and Jacob. They
were emotionally closer to me than Tante's children because Hans
and Geneviève went to a school taught in French, whereas these
two went to an American school as I now did too. They took it
upon themselves to teach me all the things that school and aunties could not. I'd sometimes stay at their house after school until
my mother finished work and occasionally would stay over for
church on Sunday. They weren't Seventh-day Adventists. Once
she'd reached America, my mother stopped caring about denom-

inations. But I remember that I was never to tell our Seventh-day Adventist aunties that I'd gone to church with "Sunday worshippers."

I never knew if Aunt Carmen had been widowed, divorced, never married, or if her man had simply stayed in place while she floated around the world for school and work like the other women. She came from Nevis, and everyone joked about how the island was so small that if you rolled over in your sleep you'd fall into the ocean. So small that every front lawn was on the beach and also every backyard. So small that you had to go to other islands to make sure you didn't marry a relative. Aunt Carmen laughed at the jokes, relishing the fact that anyone had heard of her island at all.

These two aunts would not be in my life for long, but they remain associated with two early, indelible experiences of this country. First, my encounter with America's unique relationship to skin and, second, the discovery of the song that had haunted me since the refugee camp.

The issue of skin began to encroach as my first summer in America came to an end and school approached. I could already see that there were two Americas, one white and one black. I'd still never actually met any Black Americans, no one I knew had. Still, it was emphasized to us children that despite how others might see us we were not like them. What we were was never defined except in terms of what we were not and what we did not think or what we would not do. Despite Tante and Aunt Carmen being equally emphatic about our not being Black Americans, I have no memory of their families, one Caribbean and one African, spending any time together. They were as segregated from one another as we all were from both Americas. In what would become a pattern, my mother shuttled me between Caribbean and African people in hopes that my mixed heritage would forge some notion of community in a country that seemed unable to define us as other than Black American.

Within my first few weeks of Catholic school, something happened that gave Tante the opportunity to make abundantly clear what it was that we were not. A boy my age who came from the real America, the white one, called me nigger. It was an unfamiliar word. It wasn't yet common in Jamaica or among any Africans. Because it was as alien as those rare and archaic words my mother collected, it had little impact. It was the boy's expression, the mixture of disdain and anger on his face, that told me that the word had privileged meanings. He'd expected it to have devastating effect. Up until then, the teachers and my schoolmates had seemed charmed by my accent, which seemed to me to be the thing that primarily marked my difference from everyone else. Awareness of skin color was clearly at work in Jamaica, but it hadn't yet commanded my perception of self or my sense of difference from other people. My teachers and fellow students were impressed by the way I read out loud. Here in my American school, I sought every opportunity to perform this skill, and because of it, I had already been awarded responsibility for the class library, a small bookshelf that I organized and reorganized diligently.

It was out of curiosity that I asked my mother what the word meant. I expected to make mistakes in this country, but I couldn't figure out what the boy had expected me to do in response to him or what I'd done to earn the expression on his face. Because I was new, I assumed all this was my fault. My mother gasped but said nothing. That too was proof that something unusual had happened. She seemed visibly bent by a sudden weight. She was unable or unwilling to define the word.

I was alone with the word until a few days later at Tante's house. Tante, midstream in the process of wrapping her head tie, came bursting through the door from a room where my mother had been speaking to her. With the fabric draped around her neck, she put her hands on my shoulders, delivering just enough pain from her fingernails to hold me at attention. Her children responded as if I were about to get a beating, meaning that they sat quietly assessing if they were next.

But Tante wasn't angry with me.

"Listen to me," she said. "This is very wrong and we must do something about this immediately. It is not your fault. They have mistaken you for one of the blacks. Do you get? It is because we look the same. When someone says that word to you or calls you that name, say this. *Listen*. And you must say it very well and clear. Say *I am not a slave. My father was not a slave. My grandfather was not a slave. My father's mother was not a slave. My uncles were not slaves and aunties were not slaves. We are not slaves. We came to this country by choice!*"

She turned to my mother, who had entered the room, and said, "This has happened to others of us so it is not his fault. He did nothing wrong, but it's good you all now know. This is something very important in this America, and you will be in trouble if you do not know these things." Then she turned back to me. "Now say it back to me."

I couldn't so she repeated it.

I am not a slave. My father was not a slave. My grandfather was not a slave. My father's mother was not a slave. My uncles were not slaves and aunties were not slaves. We are not slaves. We came to this country by choice!

It took at least four times before I could impress it into memory via a familiar rhythm. It helped after she told her children to say it for me. They did so easily. They'd memorized it a long time ago in English and French. Should they ever get into any trouble with white Americans, being able to call upon a French accent would be helpful. It would let them know what you were not.

She turned to my mother.

"You have to keep his accent strong. They must hear him before they see him. The whites have to know who we are so they won't treat us like them."

Aunt Carmen had been here much longer than any of the other aunties, and when she learned what had happened, she wasn't overly offended. To be mistaken for a Black American was the price of arrival, especially for children whose accents were much more vulnerable to assimilation than their parents'. Her children were older than the others so she no longer had the confidence of complete control and increasingly faced the impact of both Americas in her home. In her view, being mistaken for a Black American had its benefits. There were times when it would be good to hide within the skin, as it were. It could be safe there, and you could be left to live and prosper in this country quietly. There was no shame in invisibility as long as you knew it was not the same as disappearance.

I was too young to wonder what my mother must have thought of Tante's words. She was no longer the mythic being described in Jamaica or the hero described by Africans but a wearer of wigs. At first, I thought it was the word "nigger" that was responsible for her diminishment, but it had to have something to do with another word— "Biafra." Everything led back to that even if she wouldn't talk about it. Maybe it was because this country was also

depleted, recovering from long marches, burning cities, and violence. There had been a war here too, said Aunt Carmen, whenever any of us encountered inexplicable bitterness on the busses
or at school or in the streets. We'd arrived before they'd healed
their wounds. It was rude to expect them to attend to ours. What
I remember is that my mother told me to respond as Tante had
instructed and had me practice the words in our apartment until
they were like a song that came easily.

Armed with this catechism—it was a Catholic school after all
—I went eager to encounter that word, that boy, even that expression again. I had no greater understanding of the word itself
but felt confident that even though I'd been armed by women this
would be a manly act.

It took some days for me to find myself face-to-face with the
boy in the hallway. He was preoccupied and pretended not to
notice me. He required inciting. I remember being surprised by
how short and small he was. In the days since he'd used that word
and in the wake of my aunties' responses, he'd become taller and
threatening enough in my mind to make this confrontation seem
worthy of the courage I now felt. He remained reluctant until I
pushed him with my shoulder, causing him to stumble against the
wall. On the cusp of tears, he called me nigger again and I was
elated.

Knowing my words would carry, I spoke as much to him as for

the audience I saw gathering. It was like being on stage, a feeling that befit my being the voice of the people.

I am not a slave. My father was not a slave. My grandfather was not a slave. My father's mother was not a slave. My uncles were not slaves and aunties were not slaves. We are not slaves. We came to this country by choice!

And then I said the words again, this time emphasizing my Jamaican accent.

The boy looked up at me quizzically and began to cry. I'd said the last word "choice!" particularly loudly and wondered if that was what made him run through the hallway until he found an adult. That adult turned to see me in the hallway with the other children shrinking away from me. He marched toward me, grabbed my shoulder, and whisked me away to the main office. I felt nausea, calenture, but due to shaking on dry land, not open sea.

I was sure I would be deported, but to which country God only knew. Instead, I lost charge of the class library and was no longer given opportunities to read aloud. This wasn't so bad since my accent was no longer charming or exotic and no longer protected me from the fact of my skin. This was the punishment that turned out to be enduring: a new awareness of that skin. I'd previously thought of myself as either the only Jamaican or only African or only immigrant child in school. I now noticed that there was a handful of other black children, African Americans. If they were otherwise, they would likely have been from families my aunts would have known. I wondered if they had noticed me or thought me as invisible as they had been to me. I began to notice these things everywhere now, who was what and who looked like what and who came from where. The sounds of voices became more pressing to my ear, who had an accent and who didn't. The country began to feel smaller.

Some weeks or months later, I thought I was being given a chance at redemption. The school was celebrating Dr. Martin Luther King, and we students were each tasked with writing a poem or essay about him. I hadn't heard of Dr. King before this celebration, but regardless of how little money we had, my mother had recently purchased a more or less current set of *The Encyclopedia Britannica*, where I learned enough about him to write a poem.

I remember the first lines vividly: "Bells do ring for Dr. Martin Luther King, he made the world free for you and me."

Not only did I get to read it out loud to all the students in my grade, and thereby brandish my accent after a long silence, but my poem and performance also won a coupon for McDonald's. It was my first experience of literary notice (and I had never been to McDonald's). The following week I was asked to read my poem again in front of a larger group of students and teachers from several grades. After the reading, one of the teachers came to the front of the class. She was the only black teacher at the school I can recall, and she was livid. After glaring at me, she turned to my audience and declared that Dr. Martin Luther King was great but that he didn't die for me. He died for her people, not mine. It was wrong for me to win. Africans were backward and spent all their time killing one another, like in Uganda and Biafra, and were an embarrassment to real black people. She grabbed the poem from my hands, crumpling it.

It is hard not to tell this story alongside the one about my introduction to the word "nigger" and the sudden awareness it brought to skin and accent. I was too young to know that the teacher's view of Africans might not have been shared by other blacks and also too new to the country to acknowledge her own conflicts with this great land to which my mother and I had fled. But the fact that the conflict occurred in front of an audience of whites looking on in amusement and perhaps pity did not leave me.

The country shrunk again, smaller than Biafra and even Jamaica. At least I still had the coupon.

But, as they said in this country, timing is everything. I thought they said it because things here still happened for a reason even if God was indifferent or optional. Here everything was preordained, destined. Randomness was for countries where bodies clogged rivers and roads, and mothers left children behind.

It was in the thick of these shifting perceptions of race and accent and America that I finally found the song that had haunted me. The song about Major Tom and Ground Control, about floating in space, refusing to land. I'd hear it occasionally late at night with my transistor radio fuzzing me to sleep but never in full and never with the singer's name or song title. The night I found the song, my mother was working and I'd been left at Aunt Carmen's apartment with Karina and Jacob. Aunt Carmen was asleep in her bedroom and had allowed us to eat, play, sleep, and watch television together in the living room. The lights were out except for the television that was crowned with an antenna made of a wire clothes hanger. We lay on the floor covered with a blanket, fast-food wrappers and containers scattered around. Soda cans and cups had been shaped into a castle around us, but somehow its walls separated Karina and me from her younger brother. Jacob had recently sprained his wrist and had fallen asleep with his arm curled on his chest like an insect.

Though I'd avoided this many times before, I didn't move my hand now while Karina rubbed it between her thighs. She held me tightly enough to cause the bones in my hand to rub painfully against one another. Because this wasn't my first time rubbing like this, I was able to keep focused on the television even with its images appearing in between bursts of static. My attempts to get up and move the antenna to clear the screen were greeted with even more pressure from her thighs. I stayed in place. Some of the older girls back in Jamaica had done this with Cousin Danny and me when they needed help sleeping or after the reggae concerts in the stadium behind the house after the older boys had gone home. Once I'd even been brought into bed with a group of them and their school friends who were staying past Sabbath. Just when it was announced that Sabbath had ended, they pushed me into one of the rooms on their side of the house. As if I were a patient on a surgical table, they touched and poked and prodded me and had me touch, poke, and prod them. If I pushed too hard, I was hit across the face or one of the larger girls would hold me down on the bed and straddle me, reaching down between my legs to pull and twist, gauging how much pressure and pain a boy could take and laughing equally at my pleasures and failures.

Karina was gentler than the girls in Jamaica. She demanded nothing but my hand and its steady motion. The harder I pushed my hand, the faster she rubbed against it and the tighter she closed her eyes. She'd gone wet by then and my fingers slid easily inside her, first one then two. If I could make her sleep sooner rather than later, I'd have the television to myself. Karina had either forgotten or stopped caring that Jacob was lying next to her and that his fragile arm was close enough to touch when she arched and shook. The soda cans rattled but did not fall. Her breathing was loud but not enough to wake her mother. After less than a minute of short and sharp breaths, she was asleep next to her brother and I was able slowly to remove my hand, trailing moisture like a snail along her thighs.

After a rudimentary shift of the wire hanger, the blur of television static shaped into a smattering of applause. The camera moved back from the host to someone who stood with arms spread out as if crucified, his body draped in what I remember as glittering gauze. His eyes were hollow and his cheekbones sharply angled, giving him the emaciated look of an unfinished machine. His skin was too pale to call white. It was ghostly; you could almost see his inner workings. He had a woman's face painted vividly like a girl's doll, and when his mouth opened, it was the song, my song, about the astronaut floating in a most peculiar way with no desire whatsoever to land. My eyes welled up with tears. It had been so long and the song was still so familiar. I'd heard snippets of other songs that were likely from the same singer, but they had only proved that it was just a matter of time before this moment. Timing, again, was everything. Even an indifferent God allowed serendipity.

"Ground control to Major Tom . . . Commencing countdown, engines on."

Even my mother remembered those words. She had sung them

to me before she left Jamaica for America. The song was guaranteed to put me to sleep, she said, as it had back in Gabon, where the noise at night was due to the children crying except for the ones who sat peacefully, eyes wide open, and died. The fact that extreme hunger made one unable and unwilling to eat was a lesson she always emphasized, though I never understood what she meant me to learn from it. The flies made noise, she said, like the static of a transistor radio or the buzz of distant planes on their way to what was Biafra.

At the end of the performance, the applause was a full roar. Yet the singer didn't smile, didn't laugh or thank the audience or even bow. That impressed me. He wasn't performing for them at all. He stood defiantly in the light as if he were looking down at the audience from above that line in the sky where blue turned to black. He disappeared long before the applause stopped.

I didn't realize I had moved so close to the screen. It covered my entire field of vision. The sound was loud enough to have brought Aunt Carmen running into the room with a belt ready to swing at me, but she didn't. The house remained silent. I felt like turning around and bowing, as if I had been the one singing and raising my arms up like a messiah in front of that rapturous audience. But it wasn't my job to sing. My job was to listen and interpret.

I left the television on until the broadcasting day ended and distortion and buzz warmed the room in restless light, then turned it off so I wouldn't get distracted and forget the name of the singer or allow the feeling to fade too quickly. I wrote it down on the nearest scrap of paper. In the sudden silence, I saw Jacob still asleep and also Karina, her fingers between her thighs and the moisture now coated white on her skin. There was that imperceptible change in atmosphere, that sudden crispness that said morning was coming. For the first few minutes after the singer had gone, I'd been annoyed that my cousins could sleep through something so momentous. But this was obviously not a communal revelation. Even though they were immigrants, Aunt Carmen always reminded them that they had a home on the island of their birth and could always return. I had no such luxury. But I could claim this peculiar floating, a curse I would have to shape into my own kind of blessing.

Calentura: "calenture" in older English sources.

Cuban fever or, in colloquial terms, sexual arousal.

In the nineteenth century, the word named a species of tropical fever commonly identified among sailors, convicts, and slaves. Victims found themselves beset by a longing so powerful that it caused doctors and philosophers to make declarations about the impact of climate on culture and temperature on race. It's not surprising that such diagnoses rendered peoples from the tropics less prone to the cold balance of reason and more subject to the torpid violence of passions. This has now become merely a promise made to tourists.

One imagines calenture in line with nostalgia, also once thought to be an illness, from the Greek *nostos* (homecoming) and *algos* (pain). It was affiliated with paranoia and melancholia, other illnesses as hard to identify as they were to treat, given how patients seemed to luxuriate in the symptoms.

The symptoms, however, are far more meaningful than the condition's almost forgotten history. Calenture brought a specific kind of delirium. It was not unusual for one so afflicted to suddenly see the ocean as a vast, rolling green field, rich with flowers, brush, and familiar grass. At sea for months at a time, parched for the sight of land, sailors flung themselves into this expanse knowing that home was just beyond the next rise, sure-footing themselves to death.

As we know, many enslaved Africans chose to drown rather than remain captive. Some folktales tell us they tried to fly back to Africa, having sprouted wings from the transformative power of their longing. But in cases of calenture, this leap wasn't an act of suicide or evidence of madness. It was a final grasp at certainty, knowing that they could make their home in permanent flight.

5

Absolute Beginners (Part I)

After spending so much time rummaging through the boxes in our apartment and looking at pictures of my father and godfather in military uniforms — the latter with his notable beard on the cover of international magazines — my desire to know more about these men grew stronger. This was especially the case because actual men were still scarce in my world. My father in particular became more and more a source of fascination. I had been with my mother long enough now to know that asking direct questions about him wouldn't be easy. We had yet to develop any ease with each other that could lead to the sharing of difficult information. I still held my guard against her.

There were many images of my father in infantry school in England, where I knew my parents first met and where their story, which had become mythical in Jamaica, started. In these pictures, he was running and climbing and marching with white men. In some—I noticed now that skin had become more significant to me—he was commanding them. He and my godfather were always at the center of every picture. And the white men were always at the edges of the photos. But I could find no information in the apartment about my father's death.

I occasionally left some pictures of my father on the kitchen table or on our foldaway bed hoping to prepare my mother for an imminent conversation. She needed to know that I was curious, amassing facts. Whenever she saw the pictures or saw me looking at them, her face grew stern enough that I could tell it wasn't time to ask my questions. She was always too tired from working or always preparing to take another shift or always getting ready to take me to stay with one of my aunties and cousins or upstairs to stay with Aunt Ngozi. I looked for an opening, an opportunity. Her discomfort, anger, or pain wouldn't deter me. These would only be evidence of wounds I still wanted to inflame.

The opportunity came when I found a leather-bound photo

album clasped with a small lock. It was in an area I'd never dared look before—the space in the closet where she kept her underwear, handbags, and other personal items, the one place free of files or boxes or items branded with drug logos or the names of medical supply companies. Because the album was worn and battered, the clasp lifted right off the cover. The album opened even though the lock was intact. I saw photographs of a funeral. It didn't take long for me to realize that it had to be my father's funeral. The casket was closed, but most of the pictures featured my mother dressed in black, a veil over her face, weeping and surrounded by various people. She wore dark glasses under the veil, adding to the glamour all of those old black-and-white pictures conveyed. My godfather was in full uniform, surrounded by a military guard. I could only assume that the various women and men not in military uniform were members of my family that I could not have remembered.

Showing my mother the album had the desired effect. She slowed, then froze, sitting down heavily. It was clear she hadn't seen it for ages or, for all I could tell, had never actually looked in it since she turned each page as if it were the first time. Each new image drew a gasp or a whisper. I wondered if I'd presented the book too aggressively. Her silence suggested a hurt that even at my age and despite my resentment of her I dared not exploit.

"Who *was* he?" I eventually asked.

"This was your father," she said. "It was his funeral."

"I know but who was he?"

Her lips were open, poised on the precipice of speech, but she remained silent without even breath.

"I want to know about him, what he was like."

Something about her silence that looked like imminent speech triggered me.

"I've seen all of the pictures and read all of this stuff in the house, and I remember people saying all kinds of things in Jamaica. Was he a king or a prince or a hero? What happened to him? It was in the war, I know, but how was he killed?"

It all came from me in a great burst, a rush of questions that began softly and sincerely but quickly evolved into a series of demands. I was owed this information. I was *the first son of the first son* for God's sake. Mine was a legacy of fame and she merely its conduit.

"Was my father famous just because of the war? And my godfather, he was a hero too. Where is he now? Will he come see us? Is the war really over? Why didn't we win if we were all heroes?"

She sat there in a cocoon of silence as if she hadn't heard me. Her lips had closed, and it seemed to me she'd retreated from whatever she may have seemed ready to share. I'd expected some anger from her and hoped for some pain, but this utter lack of emotion was an unexpected move on her part.

"Why didn't we go back to Nigeria after the war? Why did we have to go to Jamaica at all?"

And with her silence now seeming aggressive, even retaliatory, I asked what suddenly seemed more important than everything else I'd purportedly wanted to know.

"Why did you leave me in *that house?*"

At that, she raised her head. She closed the photo album and looked at me with a warmth that wilted me in ways her silence didn't. This, I now knew, was the violence of women, even more reason for me to find men and escape from this city. This was the wrong America. She knew enough to not reach out to me, but her eyes were so soft that it took every bit of strength I had not to go to her.

She never answered any of those questions, and I wouldn't ask them again for years. But it was clear to me now that my mother had failed me. My aunts too. Men would have taught me the correct response to "nigger," there was no question about that. Men would have explained the various meanings of skin that were suddenly thrust on me in school after such a short time in this country.

It was sometime soon after that that I started hearing her speaking to my aunts about our leaving Washington, DC. She never told me directly why, but I overheard that we were going to Los Angeles, a city far on the other side of this endless country. There was an uncle there, a blood relative. I was excited, not about the move or the city but because he was an uncle. Maybe Los Angeles would be my city of men.

6

All the Young Dudes

The rumor was that the Bloods were planning to open fire on our school playground sometime today. That street gang controlled the area from downtown Inglewood all the way back to the Crenshaw District of South Los Angeles, just beyond where my mother and I now lived. When we'd arrived from Washington, DC, I couldn't yet recognize the hand signs, icons, colors, and other differences between the gangs that were everywhere, the Bloods, the Eight Tray Gangster Crips, or the Blood Stone Pirus. I called them all Diamond Dogs in my head in homage to the

David Bowie album of the same name. His vision of a postapocalyptic world of feral teenagers roaming the streets seemed just right. Learning to distinguish between gangs and territories was as crucial to my survival as dodging the police, who seemed unable to differentiate between gangbangers and any random cluster of black boys in the area.

Our junior high school was flanked by the concrete buildings of the Inglewood Courthouse to the north and another set of gray structures to the west. The school's location gave rise to many jokes about how convenient the site made it for students to ping-pong from building to building. Those jokes weren't completely untrue because it wasn't unusual to see friends or brothers of friends on their way to court in recently purchased suits. Just behind the school was the Inglewood Public Library, also concrete. Behind the library was the local high school, which had a reputation in line with its location in the heart of Inglewood. The stories of gang violence and mayhem at times may have been exaggerated but were eagerly embraced by us middle-school boys because they enhanced our own street credibility.

Which is why the rumor of snipers firing on our playground quickly became fact in our minds when the principal announced over the loudspeaker that we weren't allowed out of our classrooms during recess or lunch. All the boys clustered by the windows, eager to witness or claim participation in whatever was about to happen. I joined them, thrilled finally to be in a world of men.

When it came time for gym class, we filed out from the locker rooms into the gymnasium. The exercise of the day, Coach announced, was square dancing. As strange as this was, we dared not complain because Coach terrified us. She was white and a woman, and was rumored to be able to dunk a basketball. More than a few of us mumbled that square dancing was a white people thing, but Coach ignored this. She was clearly looking for a way to keep us off the playground. The dance would force the boys and the girls to engage one another. We were at the age when being coerced into dancing allowed us to maintain that feigned indifference to one another we were attempting to master. We grabbed our partners and do-si-doed and laughed at the white people's music that Coach played from a record player. I laughed louder than most because I couldn't let anyone know that country music was wildly popular in Jamaica and more familiar to me at the time than the music my American peers listened to.

After class, Coach led us through the school and outside the building as if we were having a fire drill. She set us free in front of the courthouse, where there were always police cars and officers moving in, out, and around the gray buildings that today seemed to protect rather than intimidate. My friends were waiting near the police cars with rumors about why what we'd expected did not happen. Some said the gang chose a different school. Some said they got caught or the date was wrong.

No one our age walked these streets alone. Even if we quarreled or fought, it was always understood that the walks to and from school were never forfeited. Whether we chose to go straight down La Brea or to cut through Centinela Park, it was always best to be in a group. No one wanted to be alone in case of a run-in with the Diamond Dogs; or any wannabes looking to make a name for themselves; or the police, whose intentions were always opaque; or other groups of boys or girls as afraid as we were and equally eager to prove themselves fearless.

Just as my friends and I were about to cross Prairie Avenue to the park, I realized I'd left something behind in the locker room, something no different to me than an internal organ and just as vulnerable. In a panic, hoping I was wrong, I rummaged through my bag. My friends wondered what was going on. Was it money, my house key, homework, some girl's phone number? Terrified and not daring to tell what I'd lost, I bolted back toward the school. That I would do so alone must have conveyed to the others how serious this was.

When I got back to the school, the police cars were gone, the doors closed, and the gates chained. One of the school counselors escorted me in once he saw the urgency on my face and after I told him that I had left something important in the locker room. My stomach went queasy and my eyes wet, and I was so scared that it didn't matter if anyone saw me crying. The terror came from imagining one of the older boys, or one of my friends, or one of those boys who constantly had beef with me for one reason or another in possession of what I'd lost. What I did find was the empty folder that had held what would make me more vulnerable in this community than my accent, my familiarity with country and western music, or my adoration of David Bowie. It was, or had been, my first attempt at a novel.

When my mother and I arrived in Los Angeles, we stayed with my great-uncle Irving. He was, I learned, our only blood relative in the United States. But he turned out to have been alone for so long that having family around wasn't easy for him. He was a carpenter who'd come to California after World War II and made himself wealthy building kitchens for the black middle class he'd arrived in time to see emerge. His house where we stayed for our first few months was just a block off Crenshaw Boulevard, a street that would be immortalized in gangsta hip-hop and a series of "hood" films that presaged and followed the 1992 riots, which spilled over into this very neighborhood. The house was a fortress surrounded by walls and bars. Most of the houses in the neighborhood were the same. They reminded me of Montego Bay, front porches like birdcages and yards like compounds.

Great-Uncle Irving's carpentry business was nearby on Slauson Avenue. He drove a scarred and wounded pickup truck, but on Sundays and occasional Saturdays he brought out his Mercedes Benz and made the rounds. Most important for me was the fact that in his storefront shop was a collection of pornography more varied than what my friends and I found in liquor stores. Without those magazines, puberty might have been more difficult.

Close to his house was a Jamaican grocery store on Crenshaw that sold meat patties, cocoa bread, and, if you arrived early enough on weekends, the Jamaican national dish, ackee and saltfish. This would be gone before noon, and to get it, people often resorted to behavior Great-Uncle described as "truly Jamaican," hence his refusal to eat there and his only grudgingly shopping in the store. The owners ran a proper sit-down restaurant even closer to his house. He didn't eat there either even though we could smell the wonderful odor of jerk chicken when they made it in the parking lot.

The owners of the grocery store and the restaurant had the same last name as my mother's maiden name. Rumor was that we were related, but the connection would remain unverified. Due to some feud that had started back on the island before Britain and Biafra, we didn't socialize with the owners or expect anything beyond basic business. At one point, after an acrimonious divorce, a restaurant of the same name popped up on the other side of Slauson Avenue. Two Jamaican restaurants with the same name, the same food, and many of the same people working and loitering at each split the Jamaican community. Some sided with the wife and others with the husband. Because of that ancient family feud, we were treated with the same indifference in each one and had the benefit of both. Yet the feud confirmed a stronger sense of community for me. What provides a greater sense of belonging than shared family drama, especially the kind that travels nations and continents?

Eventually, my mother and I moved to a house deeper in gang territory than Great-Uncle's house was. There was a bus that ran by my school, but to take it would leave me vulnerable to the older kids who rode it to the local high school behind the library. And I wanted to test the freedom that came with walking the route free from adult supervision.

When I first started walking to school with the boys in my neighborhood, I refused to carry a backpack or gym bag because I wanted my books to be seen. This public display was to me a signifier of arrival. It may have led to my being singled out by gangbangers for beatings but that didn't trouble me much. In the wake of the relentless mockery of my friends, though, I took notice. All this reading meant, apparently, that I was "acting white."

Bowie's music and also the reggae and calypso my family played a little too loudly on weekends drew the same accusations. Anything that was alien to my friends and neighbors was branded white even if it came from Jamaica or Nigeria. This accusation was already a strong cliché in that suburb of Black America even among those who rejected it as a racist myth. It didn't seem a reasonable insult to me because there were barely any white people to mimic. And why would I want to imitate white people? Even the ones on TV didn't read.

I remember no more than four white kids in a school of hundreds of black and Mexican kids. The few white families still in our neighborhood never interacted with their neighbors, and their children were not seen on the street. Those kids appeared only in class where they were judged as weak, to be pitied, not imitated. They may have been ensconced in "advanced" or "mentally gifted" courses, but we all knew it was because they were unable to survive on their own. White kids rarely appeared on the playground, and the girls wore their hair in rigid buns for fear that some other student would light their hair on fire. The only other whites were teachers, head coaches, librarians, and police officers, none of whom lived in the neighborhood.

Acting white, then, had nothing to do with white people or their skin. Learning this was a true revelation. Acting white had to do with how those who read spoke and how they began to react to the people and world around them. It defined a curiosity seen as dangerous because it meant you were testing this community's definitions and limits. This curiosity had to be policed, it seemed to me, because it threatened those definitions and limits by suggesting they could be transformed.

What seemed especially strange, given what I knew from being born on the African continent and having spent years on a majority-black island, was that Blackness had nothing to do with where we came from. At least not in this neighborhood. We immigrants certainly weren't Black — we were told so regularly by our neighbors and friends who were, apparently, *really* Black. If whiteness wasn't really about skin, neither was Blackness.

My accent and obsession with books also marked me as foreign, making the only manhood I could imagine — a Black one — seem out of reach. That's likely why I soon stopped reading entirely. My mother was too busy with work to notice, at least until she began hearing from the vice principal that I was getting into regular fights. One in particular featured my using a bicycle chain to strip some flesh from one boy outside the school's main gate after having driven a sharpened pencil deep into the thigh of his second in command. The police had been called. Had it not been for the fact that the boy was armed with a broken broomstick and had bloodied me, I likely would have been the only one suspended.

The refusal to read had led to a refusal to study. This led to

greater popularity with the boys in the neighborhood and greater
power in the school. I spent more time in the street and less with
my extended immigrant family, the cousins from the Caribbean
and Africa who had begun to coalesce into a not-yet-quite-Amer-
ican community.

Where my teachers, principal, and vice principal explained my
behavior via notions such as negative influences and the romance
of street life, and where my aunts and uncles attributed it to the
fact that we were no longer regular churchgoers, my mother immediately linked it to my turning away from what I'd always loved
—books. She began a campaign, bringing home novels from the
gift shops of the hospitals where she worked and making sure
I spent time at the library. She promised me anything if I read:
the latest tennis shoes, the right kind of polo shirts—Le Tigre
since we couldn't afford Ralph Lauren or Lacoste—or sharply
creased corduroy trousers (she had no idea these were what gangbangers wore). Understanding my new leverage, I insisted on her
buying a foldout record player and 45s from local department
stores. I wanted to stop depending on the randomness of radio to
hear Bowie and listen to him privately without the judgment of
others.

Still, my schoolwork continued to suffer as my notoriety began
to spread. Not reading became almost as natural as reading, and
sitting in the back of class as comforting as the fear or anxiety

I'd see in the eyes of each new teacher. I was physically matur-
ing, growing taller, wider, and stronger. Very few could guess
my age and assumed that I was much older than my friends. I
began to sprout facial hair much earlier than any of my friends or
cousins of the same age. My body was becoming less and less my
own property and more the product of everyone's assumptions.
The meanings of this physicality were made clear every day by
everyone and required time and effort to master. Reading got in
the way of that field of inquiry. My aunts and uncles began to ac-
cuse my mother of failing as a parent. I was becoming that thing
they feared most in their children — an American, or to be more
accurate to their prejudices, a Black American. They insisted it
was time for me to be sent back to Jamaica for at least a summer
as a way to correct her errors and halt the cultural contagion. My
aunts and uncles gathered a collection for the ticket. My mother
took on more hours at work and yet another job. Big Auntie and
Uncle Daddy were contacted and a date was selected.

Being called the Black American in the family was hardly an
insult. I saw it as evidence that I was achieving the kind of manhood the boys in my neighborhood feared and envied. I became
so focused on this manhood, its bodily characteristics and the relentless tests it required on the streets or in the playgrounds, that
I don't quite recall how it was that I ended up in remedial education. Most of the other boys I regularly fought with were in these

classes. My Jamaican accent was still present, and I'd gotten used to the fact that some teachers heard it less as an accent and more as a sign of mental limitations. I'd also gotten used to being treated like a problem, which only made me act more like a problem, which only made me more popular. I began to feel that there was a place for me in this culture. My mother didn't know any of this, working as hard and often as she was.

One day we were given a standardized test that focused on reading comprehension. I finished early and, as always, spent the rest of the time disturbing the other students. A few days later the teacher kept me after class. I assumed it was to complain about my behavior. Instead, she asked if I'd cheated on the test and I said no. She asked again and I said no again, aggressively, because for all the trouble I'd gotten into, no one had ever accused me of cheating. She apologized, and her tone became warm, perhaps a bit sad. She agreed. It wasn't possible for me to have cheated—I sat so far in the back of the class that I wasn't close enough to copy anyone's answers. She asked me to have my mother contact her, which I agreed to do but didn't. After weeks had passed during which I'd hoped the teacher had forgotten about the request, she set up a meeting with the vice principal and my mother.

On the day of the conference, I sat at my desk as my always-exhausted mother spoke with my teacher and the vice principal, a man who'd never paid much attention to me beyond breaking up my fights or marching me to the principal's office. The teacher wasn't angry but concerned, even emotional. Apparently, my test scores were the highest she had ever seen. The vice principal was startled, having expected that this meeting would need to result in severe disciplinary action, perhaps expulsion. My mother smiled proudly, saying that I'd always been in love with books and a strong reader, and had declared myself a writer before I'd even begun to learn how to write.

The teacher responded that this is why this was such a sad situation. This was exactly how African American boys slip through the cracks. *It is racism,* she proclaimed, that's why I was in these classes and was likely to be held back a full grade. Racism, plain and simple.

What do you mean, *held back?* My mother was shocked. What do you mean by *these classes?* (I was, of course, thrilled to be called African American.) That's when and how she found out that I'd been placed in remedial education. It was also when I realized that my being in remedial education wasn't just because of my tough-guy behavior but due also to those questions about my mental capabilities.

My mother wasn't one to cry in public. I'd seen her cry at my grandmother's funeral in Jamaica just before I moved into Big Auntie and Uncle Daddy's house in Montego Bay and when she greeted me at the airport in Washington, DC. She didn't cry at this meeting, but I saw the way she was breathing and knew how much it took for her to maintain composure. I was too big to be physically punished, but the wilting of her body and the sudden distance between us was enough to rattle me.

Seeing her that day and for all the days following — more exhausted than ever, appearing late in the evenings from work only to disappear into rooms filled with papers and fabrics, and pictures and boxes, barrels and bottles, and letters and memories — was likely what caused me finally to forgive her for leaving me behind in Jamaica years ago even though I knew she would punish me by sending me there again.

I was silent on the walk to school after a weekend spent mostly indoors. It never occurred to any of the boys I walked with to imagine that the plan to shoot up our schoolyard the week before had been a rumor or hoax or empty threat. At school the day continued as it usually did. There was no sign that anyone had found or read my manuscript but that only intensified my paranoia. The silence could have been produced by a vast conspiracy that everybody was in on. When a message came to the playground either at lunch or recess that Coach wanted to see me, I thought nothing of it beyond the likelihood that something I'd done wrong had finally caught up with me.

I met her in her office near the gym. I sat slumped, resigned to hear how I was going to be punished for whatever I'd done. I didn't notice my manuscript fanned out on the desk between us like a deck of cards.

"Is this yours?"

Her voice was as stern as usual, the voice of a woman who could dunk.

Shocked, I reluctantly said yes. Then she asked me again with more than a hint of disbelief. She leaned back in the chair and shook her head from side to side.

"You wrote that," she said incredulously. "All of that yourself?"

Yes, I told her. It's mine.

"But *why* did you write it?" Her voice became warmer.

It never occurred to me to ask myself why I wrote. Writing was simply an outgrowth of reading. I answered in a gesture typical of teenagers, a quasi-universal response to the ineffable—I shrugged.

I wondered if she'd keep my manuscript or throw it away. If she chose to do the latter, I hoped she'd be kind enough to make sure it wasn't on campus.

"Okay," she said. "You can take it. Go ahead."

I gathered up the pages quickly. Before I closed the door behind me, she called my name and said the strangest thing, the whitest of things.

"Have a really good rest of your day."

I ran to my locker to make sure I hid the manuscript before bumping into anyone curious about what I held so closely to my chest or strong enough to take it from me.

For the rest of that year, Coach said more of those strange and warm and white things: "Hello," "Have a nice day," and "Have a good weekend." She never said if she'd read or liked the manuscript or asked any specific questions about it. The fact that I'd written it seemed enough to earn her ongoing attentiveness.

One day she approached me in the middle of the playground. Angrily, loudly, she demanded I march off to her office. The fact that she continued to treat me like a thug in public was surprisingly generous. Her demeanor changed in the privacy of her office. Sitting me down, she presented me with a large box from the floor next to the desk. I opened it to find it packed with old and worn science fiction novels, including the shiny textured covers that in Jamaica were rare. It was hard to maintain my chosen persona when I saw that this collection had been curated by someone who knew and loved these books as I did. There were books I hadn't read by Marion Zimmer Bradley, Robert E. Howard, Philip José Farmer, but others by Michael Moorcock, Andre Norton, and Larry Niven were utterly new to me. There was even an almost-complete collection of Edgar Rice Burroughs's Barsoom series. I thought Coach was merely showing the books to me, but she said the box was mine. I could collect it after all of the students had left school so no one would have to see.

I was crippled with a gratitude I did not know how to express —for the books but also for the secrecy. Coach's acknowledgment of the difference between persona and self lifted a burden I'd carried alone. Her actions suggested that the space between the two would be a terrain of struggle for some time but that it was a battle that could be waged in secret and that could be won.

7

We Are the Dead

I woke again to the howling of the faceless person in the bed across from mine. Because the top of my head was wrapped like the Phantom's mask and my eye sockets were filled with cotton balls, I couldn't tell what time of day it was, but the sense of solitude expressed by the voice suggested night. I assumed it was a man, but even in the mornings, when the nurses allowed me to open my eyes, I could not discern. All I could see were bandages and exposed burned flesh. At night, I barely registered the soft light and jittery shadows of a candle. It was the nurses' station.

There was always at least one of them on duty. All the other patients were sleeping, apparently used to the noise.

He or she was tossing and turning and groaning. I knew my memory had been damaged and hoped I would soon forget hearing the screams. What it must be like to have your skin seared off and your eyelids gone. What it must be like to have every movement hurt like the very fire that caused it all. Thinking about it made my own wound tingle and a sharp pain flash across my skull. Whenever that happened, everything went blurry white and sometimes I lost consciousness. If I could have called out, the nurse would have come running, but I'd learned not to call out too often. There were patients in the ward listening for my voice. I was thankful that the pain triggered sudden, soft sleep. I don't remember dreaming in that place, even with the medication.

I was still standing because I didn't yet see the blood pooling around my feet. What I did see was Cousin Dale pointing in the direction of where the heavy tile, the kind used to lay footpaths through tourist gardens, had come from. The sharp angles probably made it more aerodynamic, sailing smoothly until it hit and turned the left side of my skull into a child's puzzle with those big pieces that are meant to be easy but end up being difficult because each piece can be forced into any other. But I didn't know this yet. I followed with a final act of concentration to where Cousin Dale's forefinger was pointing: at Garth, who stood there stunned, his mouth opened at what I must have looked like. His guilty fingers quavered and curled.

I remember wondering if the girls were still standing at the gate listening for that fine American accent I had brought back to Montego Bay and where they had watched me lord over the neighborhood like a tourist. They didn't know I'd been sent back to Jamaica as a punishment; nobody did except for Big Auntie and Uncle Daddy.

Garth bolted. The girls would have to see me try to go after him, that much I knew. But then I noticed I was standing on a red, dark, round carpet that grew wider and darker around my feet. It made sense to curl up on it and sleep.

There was a woman who was not my mother but looked like an auntie because she was watching me with concern and disapproval. I was strapped to a stretcher in the back of what was obviously a minibus and reggae oldies were on the radio. Somebody must have paid the driver a lot for my passage because there were only a few others in the minibus. The smell was familiar — working people, the kind who sat crammed together and shared bitter laughter and biting sarcasm for hours and miles and stopped for sugar cane and beer. I remember the vibration of the road and the bumps and curves around hills that put me back to sleep either due to the dizziness or sudden panic. I remember only nighttime until I awoke again on a gurney. I could make out what seemed like a market, women with packs on their heads and men with machetes and schoolchildren in uniforms. At some point, there was a quick burst of motion on my periphery. I saw matted hair, sweat, and dark skin shine, a Rastaman in rapid motion held by two men. They were trying to place him on a stretcher like mine. He resisted.

"Me nah go in deh . . . Me nah go in deh! A pure deaders in deh, and me is a living man, Selassie-I know."

This was enough to make me fall asleep again.

I was inside now, admitted to hospital. Someone said it was Kingston. I couldn't keep my head up for very long. One eye was bandaged so everything seemed filtered through gauze. I couldn't remember what had happened to me, so I assumed I was as I had always been—one-eyed, weak, easily given to calentures.

The person speaking for me was a woman, not my mother— her I would have remembered or at least I hoped that I would. They asked her if I was Jamaican because my accent didn't sound familiar. If I was to be treated as a priority, it was important to know where I was from. I wasn't American either; they could tell this even though they knew I lived there. Where was my passport? Apparently, I lived in America but was neither Jamaican nor American. Which meant that I was a citizen of this place along with the shot and the maimed and the many whose illnesses were invisible to the eye and who roamed from ward to ward. I was home.

My skull had been fractured, rearranged. This required that I move very slowly and remain in silence. The latter was impossible since this was not just the capital of Jamaica but the capital of sound. With one eye bandaged and the other unreliably open, I navigated with my ears.

Perhaps the disarranged state of my skull for those months I remained hospitalized made the bass burrow deeper and the shrieks of children sprinkle sharper. Kingston Public, the hospital I was in, was a famously loud place, abutting neighborhoods that terrified staff and supplied patients. The murmurs and groans from hospital wards and the neighborhoods became indistinguishable. I could hear music from outside, the tinny rattle of zinc on wood on aluminum making it clear that the person playing the stereo didn't earn enough money for a proper bottom end.

The nurse with light skin was the one I would trust. I was still Jamaican enough to believe that and weak enough to do so without guilt. The other nurses were just as kind, but I was no different than the other patients in being jealous of her attentions. If only I could speak properly, she would hear my American accent.

Just the sound of it could promise her things. She looked like a cousin who'd lived with us in Montego Bay while finishing secondary school. That cousin had actually become a nurse like so many women on the Jamaican side of my family. Perhaps that's why I'd gotten so comfortable in the hospital so quickly.

That cousin and her husband would visit me every few days there in Kingston and assure me that my mother was on her way but that she first had to get the money for a ticket, had to make arrangements with her multiple jobs, but that she was moving heaven and earth. What mattered was that the other patients knew it. They had to know that my mother was in America and was coming from there and that eventually I would return to America, where I was from. Word of this did spread through the wards. It spread out to the front gate surrounded by the dense market through which I'd been carried. Nurses and patients brought word that certain people had asked of me. Some sent me gifts with the understanding that I would find time to visit them once I was able. Eventually, my bedside table was littered with promises and obligations.

The first time I wet the bed, I kept my eyes closed until after I was changed and the bed refitted. I didn't know which nurse had cleaned me, but the second time it happened, it was the nurse with light skin. When she bathed me, I feared embarrassing myself with an erection. That was far too optimistic. My penis was as weak as my arms and legs. My mind suddenly went white again as if I had stared too steadily into a bright light, and I kept my eyes closed so tightly at times that they leaked tears. But the tears had no effect. She treated me as if she didn't know where I was from.

Before Garth broke my head open, we'd had a fight no different than the ones we'd had when I lived in Jamaica. The wall the tile sailed across was one we'd sat on together most nights with my cousins and other boys from the neighborhood, talking about comic books and American television programs and music. We also talked about girls. Not the ones from our neighborhood, we feared those, but the ones at school who came from towns and neighborhood in the small hills outside Montego Bay. Their social distance from us made it easy to imagine them vulnerable to our charms.

What made my conversations with Garth different this time was that I had done the thing we'd all shaped our lives in preparation for. I'd gone to America. I no longer had to make strong arguments or defend my positions. I'd also achieved a personal goal in that I'd come back as a Black American, not the African I was when I left. Every other word out of my mouth was "man"

or "cool," and I bobbed my head when I walked. I slapped everyone's palm, giving them "five," which they all gathered to receive
as if something were being passed from hand to hand.

Garth had said something, jealous of the attention I was getting. I said something back too loudly and probably too proudly.
In a flash, he'd crossed the wall from his yard and was in my face.
I had him down before he could hurt me. When he got up and
went back over the wall, I continued posing for the girls at the
front gate, ramping up the Yankee accent until I heard Cousin
Dale calling my name and raising his finger.

Gollum from *The Lord of the Rings* was hovering over me, dripping
saliva. One set of fingers was in his mouth and he bobbed from
side to side. I jerked my body when my eyes opened to him. He
pulled back and crouched down, displaying an unhealthy-looking
grin. I made to lean up but my body barely responded. The pain
in my head was too great, and it made better sense just to shake
my body vigorously.

My nurse eventually came and looked at me with professional
warmth. I wanted to tell her about the creature next to me. My
mouth was full of honey.

"You wake?"

Trying to answer her made what I'd imagined as honey pour

slowly out the sides of my mouth. Gollum smiled and crawled into the bed next to mine. He lay on his side and soon seemed to be asleep, though his eyes remained halfway open and his mouth twitched like that of a dog dreaming.

She gave me medicine for the pain and checked the state of my bed. Whenever that happened, I tried to teach myself how to make my mind go bright white and shut down everything around me. She expertly cleaned me and changed the bed. I'd forgotten why she was there.

"You will sleep good now."

Another nurse entered my field of vision with what I learned was a catheter. It was as if I were watching the procedure on TV. Better still, there was no embarrassment even when the other nurse began to tug at my penis and laugh so that my nurse had to slap her shoulder and hiss her teeth the way market women did.

At the foot of my bed was a young boy peering through the aluminum bars of the footboard. He had reddish skin and a broad smile, and seemed too short for his features and the size of his hands. He waved like he was welcoming me at the airport as I went unconscious again.

Somebody's transistor radio was on, crackly in the courtyard that separated the private rooms from the general wards. I felt the familiar rush in my chest when the strings of "Space Oddity" rose. I counted down from ten with the singer and shut my eyes tightly as he belted out the chorus. The dots of light behind my eyelids moved with the bleeps and whooshes at the fadeout.

"Phosphene." From the Greek *phos* (light) and *phene* (to show). It was one of the words my mother collected. The experience of light entering the eye, often due to head injuries or pressure or a sudden closing of the eyes leaving traces of light behind the lids. It usually appears in patterns and diagrams, sometimes kaleidoscopic or just bursts of color.

My song had come on right after ABBA's "Fernando," which had been on regular play on Jamaican radio all that summer. ABBA made me think of Boney M., also big that summer, with "Rivers of Babylon," the only reggae song allowed in Big Auntie and Uncle Daddy's house. I always confused Boney M. with ABBA, and in remembering this detail, I became buoyant because every act of remembering felt like new skin growing over an open wound.

The boy from the foot of my bed was Paul. He'd heard an American near his age was in the general ward. I was fourteen and he must have been ten or eleven. I didn't have the strength to explain that I wasn't actually an American. Also, it didn't take long to realize, even in my condition, that not to be American would mean that I was just like everybody else. This was not a place where you wanted to be just like everybody else. And it was nice having Paul run errands for me, give me information on the people in the other beds, and keep me company.

Paul didn't know my neighbor's real name and began calling him Gollum as well. He'd never heard of *The Hobbit* or *The Lord of the Rings*, but when I told him the story, he began to bob up and down like a grasshopper on his unnaturally bent legs.

Paul said Gollum had been a farmer, one of those old men always cutting with a machete at the roots of something. In a cane field one evening, he—bent over and chopping in a blind line through the sugar cane—leaned head first into a country road just as a car sped by. Gollum's senses were severely addled. Though he never spoke, there were times when he made drawling sounds as if he were sipping hot soup, or expelled hoarse, brittle expulsions of breath. His eyes gaped as if in permanent surprise, and his face was split by a grin too wide to suggest laughter. He'd been in the wards for some time, and people wondered why he wasn't in Bellevue where mad people went.

Paul's story was sadder in the way that violence done to children always is. He seemed almost a dwarf, but when I was able to sit up, I noticed his legs, bent permanently, and although he walked in a crouch, he shuffled as fast as anyone could walk. He looked like a grasshopper at first but then, I thought, like a satyr

from Greek mythology. Unlike the other patients, he never answered any questions about his injuries. No one ever came to visit
him.

I learned his story from a tall, very dark man in the wards who
also wanted to spend time with the American. The fact that I was
a boy meant nothing to him. Being American implied a knowledge of a range of topics and concerns. He spoke with the kind
of Jamaican English that had a recognizably British lilt. He spoke
like my mother.

This man was always on the patio outside the nurses' station. It
was a popular spot for patients because it had a vista of a city, albeit of cardboard, that stretched as far as the eye could see. Though
the cardboard city was more than enough to capture attention, his
face was equally brutal and fascinating. It had been burned with
acid, through the skin in places, by someone he referred to as a
business partner. His cheeks and lips looked like a candle melting.
There was only one eyebrow and the opposite eye drooped low.
He reminded me of the comic-book hero Jonah Hex, whose face
had been half melted off.

When I introduced myself, he made a gesture that I eventually learned was a smile. I tried to tell him that I wasn't actually
American but that I wasn't Jamaican either. He made that strange
twisted gesture with his face again and began laughing.

"You don't know where you come from, boy? Then you are

the luckiest person in this place." He laughed so much that he seemed to cause himself pain.

The man told me that Paul had been hamstrung by his own father. I didn't know what that meant. The boy's father had cut his son's hamstring muscles with a kitchen knife and left him on the floor to bleed.

Because no one ever visited Paul, it was assumed that his mother was not around or not interested. This was why, even though there was nothing more they could do for him at the hospital, they let him stay. Jonah Hex thought that someone in Paul's family was paying the hospital to keep him or maybe it was the nurses in the ward. Some of them took payments from people for all kinds of things. If it hadn't been for his business partner who'd stolen all of his money, he himself would be in a private room.

"Why aren't you in a private room?" he asked. "You are an American."

This as we watched near-naked women stepping over mounds of garbage as they bathed in the heat of morning. I remember their children playing with those mounds and competing with dogs for things I couldn't make out from the patio. Shirtless men would stalk by, some with radios, some with machetes. What surprised me more than their indifference toward the naked women was their general lack of interest in us on the patio. Even the near-naked women paid us no mind. I felt embarrassed for spying into their lives and hoped one would catch me. I couldn't decide what was the greater insult, their refusal to be pitied or their indifference to my desire for attention.

I woke to warm droplets of rain on my face. Maybe I was back where I'd come from. I was sure it was warm there, not humid like the hospital but with a softer heat that made things heal fast. I remembered that I was on summer vacation instead. This brought back images of school, boom boxes, and long smooth streets — America. I felt ready to remember everything, like I was about to break the surface of water from below or, better yet, like a sailor lost at sea who finally sees the water itself as land and has just hurled himself into it only to be awakened by the absence of ground. Just as I hit the water, there came the familiar sounds of Gollum now louder than the burn victim across the way. I turned my head to see Gollum pulling at his groin. He was grinning but he was in pain. He was pulling out his catheter. Urine was spraying all around him. I could see nurses running toward him. Paul rushed to my side and took off his shirt. He wiped my face with it.

When you lose your memory, your mind works to rebuild itself, offering flashes and glimpses of events and faces, sounds and echoes of words and ideas. These eventually repeat until they seem not to repeat at all. That's what we call knowledge, endless repetition, the illusion of continuity.

But when you lose your memory, there is nothing but space between those images and sounds and echoes. The rewarding part is that when those bits and pieces start reappearing you get to choose which you want to keep and which you don't. You can teach yourself to forget—at least for a while. You feel better than you've ever felt because you're choosing only the memories you like. The empty spaces aren't threatening because they are where the unpleasant memories go when you scream out or do anything to trigger the pain in your head that brings back the flashing lights behind your eyelids. Also perfect is the fact that you don't realize this is temporary. Not only are you your own creation, you are eternal.

This I know for certain.

One day Paul took me careening through the hospital court-yard out onto the slanted walkways that led to the building's front gate. I know it happened because I remember the blue-green walls giving way to pure gray concrete and the moment when I sud-denly saw the throng of higglers and market people gathered and pulsing like a singular octopus. More than likely, Paul was moving much slower than I experienced it. I would have had to be on a gurney. I don't remember any wheelchairs in that place, at least not in the general wards. Maybe in the private rooms.

I don't know how or why he wheeled me outside. Maybe the nurses had asked him to move me to or from a doctor's office, or maybe they wanted me to have some sun. Maybe I asked him, or maybe he just stole me for a few minutes and used the gurney to move as fast as he no longer could on his own, thanks to his father.

The hospital was an island of calm compared to all I could see now mottled and bright and spreading so far that just to look at it was enough to make me feel like sleeping again. What really scared me was Paul's idea to introduce me to the stall owners and itinerant sellers who sent comic books and mangos, coconut candy, gifts, notes, and questions to my bedside. They'd been waiting for me to confirm our intimacy.

Paul couldn't understand my anxiety or why I told him to stop. He kept moving, his face joyous and laughing. I screamed out and he finally halted. Paul was frightened now, thinking I was hurt and that maybe it was his fault for taking me so far outside when I wasn't healthy enough. I let him think that, twisting my face and panting even more. I also let him think that he could get into serious trouble for wheeling a bedridden patient into the market.

He began crying as he pushed me up the rise back into the hospital.

I was in tears too. I'd conjured phantom pains in my head that became real enough to induce vertigo. When the pure gray concrete became blue-green again, I relaxed my face and stopped groaning and panting. Paul was still terrified, pushing the gurney as fast as those forever-bent legs could manage through the outer ward, across the courtyard, and toward the nurses' station. I was back in bed faster than I could process it. When I looked for Paul, he was gone. He was gone for days. When he returned, it was with a letter for me from someone at the gate. Paul hadn't opened it, but if he had, he wouldn't have been able to read it because he was illiterate.

The letter said:

"My friend, I am not happy you have not come to see me after all this time. You have been here for weeks now, and I sent word through the nurses and this crippled boy who I know is your friend and loyal. They say you are not remembering well, but you must know me because I have sent you some things. We are going to be great friends. We have much to discuss before you leave to America. It would be rude of you to leave before that, my good friend. Do not forget me."

I was angry because of the letter's intimacy. My return to the island had already taught me that sometimes people claim to be hurt by you as a way to claim you.

Jonah Hex sat down next to me on the patio. There was enough of a breeze for his sheets to make a slight noise when they moved around his body. I may have forgotten his real name but I remember his smell. Paul had bought me some biscuits from the market. I offered one to Jonah Hex even though watching him chew was enough to keep me from eating. Mercifully, he declined.

Another patient was on the patio, paying no attention to the beehive of the cardboard city across the road. Through the corner of my eye, I saw him use his shoulders against the wall to stand up and do an odd and prolonged shuffle that set him by my side. I assumed it was my Americanized accent that brought him. He smiled broadly in my face, smelling much stronger than Jonah Hex. His visible foot was so dirty that there was no distinction in color between the sole and dark brown flesh, but the other was just a bandaged stump. As he smiled at me up close, I saw that his tongue had been cut out too. The restless mound of remaindered flesh moved when he tried to speak.

He quickly became hard to ignore. The more I smiled patiently at his grunts, the more emphatic he became. I began to talk to Jonah Hex about America, hoping this man would go away. The more I tried to keep up the conversation, the more physical the man became, his hands on my shoulders, his breath now moist on my skin. He was trying to communicate but I was too afraid to be patient.

He soon put both hands on me. He grabbed my head and turned my face toward his, grunting louder and louder.

Jonah Hex jumped off his stoop and gathered up the excess fabric like a Nigerian uncle. With one long, muscled arm, he hit the man across the face hard enough that there was no mistaking the sound. The man fell on the ground in front of me and Jonah Hex leaned over him, pummeling his face with the same arm while the other held his robes and sheets out of the way. There was blood from either the man's mouth or nose or both. Jonah Hex stopped when two nurses reached the patio.

"This fool was attacking our American. And nothing nah go so. You hear?"

The nurses seemed to understand immediately. Without words, they picked up the man with no tongue. His whole body shuddered the way that left-behind piece of severed tongue did when he spoke. They took him into the ward.

"Go on, boy, keep talking. Tell me some more."

I owed it to him but also to the people across the road who were watching now and were gathered at the edge of the fence. I kept talking, louder and louder. They could finally hear me.

* * *

On the day my mother was coming, I woke up early. She would have reached the island by breakfast. She would have flown directly into Kingston, not Montego Bay, and taken a taxi straight to the hospital. Paul was on the lookout. He was as excited as I was and had begun telling stories about what she would do when she arrived that were more colorful than my own. What woke me was the very memory that she would be arriving. I'd held the memory for days. I was getting better. Things were staying with me longer. I no longer feared memories dissipating like the sounds of the ward that I made sure to forget before I'd healed enough to lose control over my ability to make my mind turn bright white and shut down.

I'd slept the whole night through for the first time since my surgery. It was a strange sensation, uneasy. Gollum was sleeping with his eyes open as usual yet something was different. The ward was the same, the nurses, the smell of full bedpans and disinfectant and the shuffling sound of Paul doing his rounds. It took some time to realize what had changed. The bed across the way from me was empty. The bed was made and turned down expectantly for someone else. The bandaged man or woman had died in the night. Though I witnessed him or her so long in so much pain, it never occurred to me that he or she would die. At a certain point, the bandaged patient had become merely a reminder that pain was permanent and that we would all simply continue this way.

Whoever came for the dead had come while I slept. It had been the first night of real silence. The only noise now was the righteous *bangarang* of the Kingston morning.

8

This Is Not America

I came back from Jamaica scarred and scared, done with the island because it seemed done with me. During my absence that summer before starting high school, I'd lost a friend to gun violence and two others to prison. And while I was away, my mother had decided to send me to a Catholic high school in a white neighborhood near the airport.

In junior high school, I had started to take sports seriously. Being on a team was like being in a gang—the same level of protection from the streets but with more respect from the wider community. Football was particularly useful, but it didn't insulate me from all claims on my loyalty. Some of the homies I used to walk with to and from junior high now spent most of their time on those same streets, migrating between petty squabbles with one another and interactions with the police. Whenever I saw them, I had to prove myself in some way. This led eventually to my agreeing to let them into the gym one evening when the school was closed. All first-string ballplayers knew where the key to the storage room was kept. My friends moved in and stole sports equipment. I didn't take anything but we were all caught and I had to face a disciplinary hearing.

My mother rounded up all the white friends she had from the hospitals where she worked to testify to the school disciplinary board on my behalf. Not only did these women sing my praises, they all also emphasized that I read books, a lot, and how remarkable that was and that I wasn't really American, I was an immigrant and so easily swayed by natives because I didn't know much better but would learn because I read books. In the school and eventually in my neighborhood, the fact that I wasn't expelled was enough evidence that I'd snitched on my friends. Plus, word had gotten out from the disciplinary hearing that I read books, a lot.

My punishment, being cut from the football team, meant I'd lost everything—reputation, protection, the promise of sex. Being branded a snitch meant I was not only ostracized by my friends but also had to keep watch over my shoulder. The only people I could occasionally socialize with were the friendless white kids with weird hair who read science fiction and listened to rock music and loved, yes, David Bowie. With no social group, I found myself in the library during recess and lunch. In a dingy office behind the library, I eventually discovered the college guidance counselor.

But the effects of that discovery would not play out in my life for another couple of years. I needed immediate help. The only person I could turn to was a cousin who'd been sent back to Jamaica himself multiple times though he seemed immune to the punishment. Cousin Brian had arrived in America years before me, long enough ago to have utterly lost his Jamaican accent. That alone made him a hero to many of my cousins. On top of that, he'd become a legend in the neighborhood while a cautionary tale in the family. He had played sports for a time too until he found his greater loyalty. He had by now spent as much time in as out of jail. He'd become a Diamond Dog and his reputation was such that merely mentioning his name in certain areas of the city could save us cousins from a serious beatdown.

Even though his parents had achieved the American middle class in record time, this was Inglewood, which meant street life was still close enough to make gang life attractive to a "pretty boy" like him. Middle-class boys rose quickly up the ranks not only because of their tendency to overcompensate for their privilege through violence but by the fact that their parents could afford lawyers. His mother had been friends with mine from when they were both nursing students in England during the 1950s. His family may have been among the most successful of the families, but if you asked others, those who heard the fights between Cousin Brian and his father that ended with slammed doors or the thud of bone on flesh or bone on bone, he was headed for prison the whole time. He had always displayed open disdain for our families' habit of cultivating foreignness. When a rumor came up that he had actually been born in the United States, my uncles and aunts allowed it to continue out of resentment toward him for the disdain he showed them. But after he went to prison for the final time, we young cousins kept him in our family by dismissing the rumor as absurd.

Cousin Brian was often blamed for my own propensity for violence. He had taught me that violence was its own method of belonging or at least of finding a space that was yours in a neighborhood that my cousins saw as permanent and my elders insisted was temporary. He introduced me to the idea that the difference between a strong man and weak one wasn't physical strength or skill but ultimately the will to do violence and that this could be cultivated. It became easy for me to transfer that will to the football field or basketball court, especially since games often ended with actual violence in the parking lots or on the long walks home.

Cousin Brian was old school to the bone even as guns were entering our field of play. Only employ weapons you were born with, he said. They hurt if you use them incorrectly and thereby limited their own use. Ironic, since guns were the weapons of choice that night at the motel on La Brea where the bodies were found and from where he fled until he was either caught or surrendered and went up for double homicide (at that point, all details were suppressed as his mother and father stopped uttering his name and used the intensity of their denial to keep us from talking about it).

It made sense to seek him out now. It was a surprise to see him open the door, boyish face smiling in a way that made me wonder at times if his good looks had something to do with his need to overcompensate with toughness. Nothing was worse in that part of town than being a pretty boy. There was his general refusal to comb his hair even though he—as was still the style—kept an Afro pick in it, the type with a Black Power fist on the end. As much as he adhered to the style codes of his street family, his natural good looks made those styles seem affected. His body had changed since his last prison bid. It was more muscular, at least the torso and arms, almost grotesque in contrast with that face. In a few weeks or months, he would be gone for good, his name then able to confer to us cousins the respect that came from having a relative doing heavy time.

I'd started lifting weights myself at the local YMCA. Not only because of sports but also because I wanted to look capable of the kind of violence I was no longer willing to commit. My mother had paid for the membership on my return from Jamaica, hoping it would keep me out of trouble. Cousin Brian approved the difference in me as he took me into the garage where there was a rickety workout bench with weights and a boom box without a cover and a tape shoved in. The cassette had to be removed when necessary by a butter knife.

He asked a question, one he'd asked me when I had first arrived in LA. Was I the king of my school? I'd had no idea what he was talking about back when I was new to this city. I'd heard older boys on the basketball court debating who was or wasn't king of the school but never paid this much mind. The king of a school, I eventually understood, was the boy who could whoop everybody's ass or—and I learned this later, not from Cousin Brian but from what happened when I became a contender in this game—people *thought you could*. The distinction was significant.

I said no to his question in the garage. That guns had moved from lore to reality made his type of manhood less appealing to me. I wanted to tell him that I'd come to realize something that he'd never pointed out, that each fight could now lead to death and that I now knew people who had died. Also, my head had been broken open in Jamaica. It was filled with awful images and feelings of such weakness that I couldn't conjure up that wild breath in my chest that he'd taught me to enjoy before swinging my fists or while taking a blow. When I'd first arrived in Los Angeles, I'd said no to his question as well and his mentoring began in earnest. Those first few tutorials consisted of his beating me until I no longer feared being beaten, the lesson being that nobody at my school could hit this hard so no one was worthy of fear.

On this visit, I tried to speak to Cousin Brian about my time in the hospital in Jamaica, what I'd seen and what had led me there, but also my return and the new confusion about who I was and was supposed to be. I tried to speak to him for the first time about my alienation from my family and my friends, about the Jamaican accent that still flickered even as I struggled to keep it hidden. How had he so completely lost his and what was it like to have crossed over and become one of them? We'd never had this kind of conversation before, but high school without the protection of football was no joke and I was terrified. He was the "Black American" in our family, and I needed some insight about how he had become one, how he had assimilated and become a man.

I took in every word, every shrug and gesture, and even every moment when he punctuated his points by moving the Afro pick around and patting his hair back into shape. If what he taught me could be reduced to words, it would be something like this. Gang life was his America, a small enough piece of it anyway for him not only to manage but also control. He'd met other black immigrant kids in that world, Belizean, Eritrean, Caribbean. Like them, he'd assimilated head on without the parry and thrust or denial and blame that the rest of us depended on. Our vacillation was the problem. Inbetweenness was weakness, *pussy*. There could never be doubt about where he stood, where he belonged, what side he was on. He aimed to be certainty itself, reality personified. You'd think this would enable stillness, a quiet coming from absolute self-knowledge. It was the opposite. It required a relentless generating of fear in others to keep them on edge and render a man's history and authenticity beyond reproach.

"Accent doesn't matter, racism doesn't matter, white people don't matter. Nigerian, African, Caribbean don't matter either," he said. "We—our people—are stupid to hold on to those types of things. That's why people hate us."

In his view, only one black identity mattered in America and there was no point in fighting it or asking it to recognize ours because we would always be secondary to it. This was their country, their game. But as if he wanted to make sure I wasn't utterly disconsolate at his revelations, he said there was, however, a way to win.

"Become king" was what he said, over a cassette gone squeaky at the end of the tape's run. It might have been the Gap Band or Zapp featuring Roger. Maybe it was Egyptian Lover. Maybe it was Prince. I remember thinking how cool it was for someone with such masculine street cred to blast Prince, who was mocked by everyone in those days as effeminate and wannabe white.

Being king required that you so master their rules that you would disappear, all traces of foreignness gone. But then you could use your mastery to rise above those who'd established the rules in the first place. This advice would stay with me throughout high school and into college, as would the fact that it came from a man on the verge of doing serious time in prison.

Despite Cousin Brian's disdain for our foreignness, his family was at the center of our Black immigrant world. His parents were my aunt Pansy and uncle Owen, and we all gathered around their dining table, usually after church when the spiritual demands of the sermon generated a hunger for a community of people untroubled by the smells that stayed on our clothes or by the ratio of spice to food. These gatherings were even larger on native holidays—Jamaican or Nigerian Independence, Carnival, Crop Over, or Boxing Day.

I began to pay more and more attention to these people who

gathered around the dining table now that high school and the road between home and school had become less and less hospitable. In addition to our ever-extending family, the table was where any black immigrant who turned up in Inglewood or South Central for educational, professional, or questionable purposes would find themselves welcome. This was also when my reading began to switch from science fiction to so-called serious literature due to all the time I was spending in libraries. It was around then that I first discovered the word "diaspora."

Diaspora was one of those words from my mother's "word of the month" or "word of the week" subscriptions. What made it stick out was that I heard it repeated around the table. The word meant the scattering of a people across different lands and countries and languages. To me, this meaning seemed immediate, oppressively intimate. It wasn't just about the Middle Passage and slavery in the New World. It wasn't even about our more specific migration from Africa to Jamaica to America. It was accents and curses, uncles and aunties, cousins and endless trips to Western Union, and obligations of all kinds. Diaspora was mapped across the plates of ackee and saltfish, fried dumplings, escoveitch fish, and curry goat.

Everyone was there, or I should say *everywhere* was there. Though still in Inglewood, the dining table was a few blocks, a hill, and an entire tax bracket away from where my mother and I lived. It was Jamaicans mostly, but there were also folks from other islands, like Aunt Viola who came from Nevis. She was somehow related to Aunt Carmen in Washington, DC, and her island of birth inspired the same jokes I'd heard in Washington—Nevis being so small that you slept in your swimming clothes because if you turned over at night you might drown or the ones about sand always being in your food or having to leave the island to avoid incest. Like Aunt Carmen, Aunt Viola laughed louder than anyone at these jokes no matter how often they were repeated. Little island/big island humor was a part of the Caribbean sensibility, and because she had married an African American, she treasured anything that confirmed her status within that sensibility. Maybe her husband didn't care for foreign blacks. He never came to the table, and when we visited Aunt Viola's house, he descended into the basement. Because of this, we never had to call him uncle. But because his children were always at the table—for a time anyway, before the older ones lost their accents and the younger ones grew confident enough to mock ours—they were still cousins.

Due to my mother's efforts, there were always Nigerians at our gatherings, particularly people she'd known from Biafra or had gotten to know after arriving in America. Our last name and my father's reputation drew many to her. Even a few Hausa people, the ethnic group responsible for the attempted genocide that brought us here in the first place, broke bread with us. In these cases, the war was never really discussed. If ever it was, it wasn't described as a national or personal or ethnic tragedy but an African or a colonial one. That way blame could be evaded and the experience shared.

Much of what our elders discussed at these gatherings was about what had triggered their migration in the first place—colonialism and revolution and independence. I paid more attention to these conversations than most of my cousins because it was likely that my godfather would be mentioned, or my father, and then the adults would all look in my direction with solemn expectation. I was still the first son of the first son, though that seemed a far less portentous state of being than when I first arrived in Jamaica.

At times, it seemed to me that these people at the dining table, as mundane as they may have appeared to most Americans, were heroes too. They had played a part in some great world-building drama that seemed epic by virtue of the fact that so much of it had failed. These elders at the table had experienced things I was beginning to read about. Revolutions, coups, exile, refugees, betrayal, starvation, genocide. Loss—what should have been and almost was—was always the tone of the conversation.

What they had failed at was freedom. That failure brought them to the shores of the Pacific Ocean and turned them into semi-inebriated uncles and embittered aunts struggling to keep control of their children. I can guarantee they'd all expected to end up in London. My mother used to say that we'd turned left over the Atlantic Ocean when we should have turned right.

Eventually, South Africans began to appear at the table. It was the anti-apartheid moment, Africa's last chance, Uncle Owen often said. We accepted these people, extending the borders of community farther and farther. This wasn't due to any romantic notion regarding common Africanness but because of what those people were not—American—and, of course, their ease with that ratio of spice to food. Not only South Africans, but Ghanaians too and a few Liberians would stop by. It was a diaspora mapped by the sound of accents—West African and Caribbean but also British, Canadian, American, and the cadences of us younger ones ranging all over the map. There would always be someone with an even more authentic tongue than those who corrected and attacked us for sounding too Yankee (to the Caribbeans) or *oyinbo* (to the Nigerians). If the outside world was where my Jamaican accent was still enough to merit comment and require masquerade, these events were where I was encouraged to keep it alive. That was how we were sure not to disappear into the vortex of American racial meanings and cultural expectations. This was, of course, counter to what Cousin Brian and some of my other cousins thought we should do, but we held our tongues until we were old enough.

What gave our diaspora shape wasn't so much racism, slavery, or the contrastive presence of white Americans. It was the more pressing reality of Black Americans. American Blacks inevitably became the topic and the source of most arguments. If Black Americans often seemed fixated on white America, black immigrants seemed fixated on Black America, as if it were the wall between them and the promises of this country. Sometimes the conversation began by someone fresh to the country discussing problems they were having with a coworker, or a schoolmate, or an unruly neighbor. Before questions were asked, the seasoned veterans would share a smirk of recognition, knowing that the person being complained about was not white. It was time to school the newcomer on what really went on in this America and that there were two Americas, two distinct regimes of pain and promise.

Things would usually begin with the newcomer asking a familiar but always loaded question, *What is wrong with Black Americans?* Occasionally, one of us young cousins would attempt to defend or explain those Black Americans to our elders since we were the ones who knew them best and spent most of our time in the crucible of assimilation. These attempts were inappropriate for interrelated reasons. First, we were not to speak back to our elders, a sure sign that we were assimilating in the wrong direction. Second, in speaking on behalf of African Americans, we inevitably slipped into their dialect, which was enough to invalidate our opinions and earn a cuff to the head.

One cousin, Lloydie, had migrated to England as a child and come to stay in Los Angeles in his twenties. Folks in our neighborhood had a very hard time believing his accent wasn't affected. Where our Caribbean or West African accents could elicit laughter, his brought threats of violence. At a local restaurant once, the Black American waitress wouldn't serve us until he started talking in his "real" voice. She had a point to make, stronger than our hunger. We ended up eating somewhere else. A few times we were even threatened by gangbangers on the street who were convinced Cousin Lloydie was talking down to them. Had we not dropped the name of Cousin Brian, we would have been bruised.

There were consolations. Local girls found Lloydie's accent irresistible. Sadly for me, I could never pull off the full English, only the occasional hint of it. That hint didn't come from England, though. It came from my mother, who, no matter how far she'd traveled from Jamaica to England to Nigeria to America, always maintained that type of British accent produced in its colonies. This drew Indians to her when they worked together in hospitals because they recognized it too — *more English than the English,* as the old cliché went. Her accent rendered her less foreign when she arrived in Nigeria in 1963 just after independence. She was no longer a Jamaican woman, something few of them had any knowledge of. She was the much more familiar *English* woman, easier to position and ultimately to accept.

As a colonial product, she manifested a prejudice typical of her generation: there was to be no Jamaican dialect—*patwah*—in the house. This put her at odds with aunts and uncles who only needed to hear Byron Lee or Bob Marley or burn their tongue on Jamaican peppers to start trembling the room with what's now called Jamaican English or just Jamaican. They were from the same class as my mother, but she had grown up on the outskirts of Montego Bay and left before the shift that began in the 1960s to claim the language of the poor as the sound of the nation. She left Jamaica before "the ghetto won," as Great-Uncle Irving would say, meaning before reggae.

My mother was the least likely to accept the blind generalizing about Black Americans common at the dining table. Because of her time with my father, my godfather, and the inner circle of the Biafran secession, a form of racial consciousness had seeped into her colonial British self. Biafrans, at least their leaders, thought of themselves as ultimately fighting an anticolonial war, a war of African liberation. She may have been skeptical of the generalized romantic ideas of African identity spun in Jamaica after she left the island, but she was also less interested in the what-is-wrong-with-Black-Americans debates here in America.

As a result, she usually chose to employ the abstraction "Black people"—initially as a corrective but eventually as a compromise. *What is wrong with Black Americans?* became *What are the struggles facing Black people? Don't trust African Americans* became *Some Black people can't be trusted.* It was a way of using an imagined global community of Blacks to mediate the unpleasant details of personal experience. By the time I began to employ phrases like my mother's in college as I became radicalized in my race consciousness, I did so fully acknowledging that they were products of desperation. Neither of us could tolerate the alternative.

In contrast to the use of racial abstractions was Great-Uncle Irving. He was an expert on Black Americans, he boasted. Evidence of this was the fact that he exclusively dated light-skinned Black American women, many of whom he would take on cruise ships, which is where he spent much of his retirement. Black Americans were just like Jamaicans, he claimed; they needed white people more than any other people because without them they wouldn't exist. But when it came to racism, he argued, there was a special intimacy between Black Americans and whites. We should stay clear of it because there was little room for others in that relationship. They couldn't see or feel anything beyond the wound that had brought them together.

Great-Uncle Irving's accent was the strangest of any of ours. He claimed it was because Angelenos had spoken differently when he first arrived in the forties. He sounded like a Jamaican countryman straining to talk like a World War II newsreel or like the men in boxy suits and women with hairstyles so angled that they seemed made of plaster who appeared in black-and-white films. Apparently, he was one of my relatives who'd been dead set against my mother marrying an African and moving to Nigeria back in the late 1950s, so all talk of Africa sent him into a rage. He also made no secret of his hatred for his home country: that's why he'd come to Los Angeles before anyone else had even heard of the place. Everybody else was going to London, some to New York, then to Miami and Toronto. Los Angeles had no snow and was as far away as he could go in America from Jamaicans and damned islands. For a while, it was paradise.

My Aunt Joy brought other ideas about accent, identity, and community to the dining table. She was a Yoruba who lived the furtive life of a second wife in a country where polygamy was illegal and shameful. Her husband never came to these events, living as he did with his senior wife and primary children on one of the best streets in upper-middle-class Baldwin Hills. Aunt Joy found all talk of "Blackness" or "Black people" alternately touching and comical. Sad also, because of how obsessed Caribbean people and Black Americans were with skin color and how far they would go to claim and defend something she thought meaningless and exaggerated. White people, well, it was obvious that they were a certain way, but Black people? What did skin have to do with anything? African Americans were Americans. The "African" part was just denial. And if there was anything that linked Jamaicans to Black Americans, it was that their assertions of pride were so relentless that they could only be masks for shame.

Her English was no different than it would have been had she been in a market in Lagos. She was one of the few people I knew who went back to Nigeria every year and had been doing so since the war ended. Sometimes she spoke pidgin, which embarrassed her son. His accent was the most African Americanized of all of ours, which deeply embarrassed his mother.

And there were others, too many to recount, uncles and aunts and cousins and friends — Uncle Tommy from Scotland with his string of white British wives, Jean-Bernard from Haiti with his Senegalese wife who apparently spoke a Parisian sort of French, an uncle from Gabon whose family had sheltered us after we'd left the refugee camps during the war — all coming in waves, going in gusts, some strong enough to have directly shaped my personality and others whose impact was brief but still important. Sometimes it was a fist to the stomach, a crude joke during prayers, a lie I had to bear. Other times it was a story I would claim as my own or fumbled attempts at sex during sleepovers. So many stories and people in this world of the dining table that was in but not of Inglewood and Los Angeles.

When the table grew too small and we too many, the younger

cousins would migrate to a satellite. At Aunt Pansy and Uncle Owen's house, that second table would be a few steps down from the kitchen where the adults sat into what was called the family room, which was ironic since generally no one was allowed in it. It was where Uncle Owen went when he wanted to be alone, which was often. A few times he hosted visiting low-level Jamaican political figures there, sometimes a South African gentleman who owned a dry cleaners on La Brea and became a stand-in for Nelson Mandela or Steve Biko at these family events. When he visited the dining table, we younger ones were allowed to sit at the edges of the room and applaud with the big folks as he talked about the imminent end of apartheid and the final freedom of Africa. This man also spoke at churches or local Black culture festivals. It was almost enough to allow him to forget how he was treated by people in the neighborhood who made a royal mess of his shop and used his parking lot for criminal and ungodly purposes.

When separated from the louder adult conversations, our individual dramas were in free play. In the absence of his mother, Aunt Joy's son could go on with his "nigger this" and "nigger that," and hold his crotch in impersonation of the kids in his neighborhood. He regaled us with tales of "bitches" and "whips," "punks" and "getting money," and poured scorn on those of us still in thrall to African or Caribbean identities. He and his mother lived very close to an area of La Brea everyone called the Jungle, which was west of Crenshaw and below Baldwin Hills. It was eventually re-named Baldwin Village due, I think, to the racial slurs inherent in the previous name.

In alternate summers, two of Uncle Owen's nieces visited from New York. All of us cousins became susceptible to the volatile mix of sex and adolescent emotional turmoil that their visits in-duced. We called them the Twins. They were not the same age nor did they even vaguely resemble each other (one was tall and string-bean lean, the other rounded like a breadfruit) but they echoed each other when laughing and talked together in a dia-lect that seemed entirely of their own devising. Though born in Jamaica, they were New York City through and through. They lorded it over all of us by repeating how much they missed Amer-ica and how they couldn't wait to get back there and how back-ward we were in terms of music and clothes and slang. To this day, I don't know if they were being funny or just had a terrible sense of geography.

If they and Aunt Joy's son were the least political of the cousins, I was the most, or became so. By the time I graduated to the main table, I began challenging everyone, using Black Americans—I insisted they be called African Americans—as my trump card. Eventually, my only reason for going to these meals was to argue. It was me, angry and alone, defending Black America against all comers and wishing that those I spoke for could witness it and finally bid me welcome.

I often made the mistake of thinking the silence around the table was defeat when, in fact, it was disappointment. Nobody actually read my anger as political, not Uncle Owen, a strict behaviorist (I recall in detail his lectures on B. F. Skinner over dessert); or Great-Uncle Irving, an absurdist in the mode of Ionesco if ever there was one; or any of the others. Not even those who were focused on politics in the Caribbean or Africa since these elders generally thought of race in America as a distraction. For them, my militancy was simply a lack of gratitude. I'd forgotten what we had left behind.

I eventually stopped going to Uncle Owen and Aunt Pansy's house. I rarely saw my cousins. When my mother hosted meals, I'd either lock myself in my bedroom and listen to music ("Studying," she told everyone. "Studying well hard.") or go out somewhere with friends ("School meeting," she'd say. "The boy is deep in his books."). Stressing my studiousness was a way of promising that I was going through a phase. That angered me more. My refusal was a protest, and I wanted it recognized. Sunday evenings I would always be sent leftovers to eat alone in silence. It was a cruel reminder that I was still one of them.

But my boycott of the dining table wouldn't last. Too often

I would be reminded that in the real America my emotional affinities and political identifications were a one-way street. Black America didn't necessarily reciprocate my sentiments, and the fact that white teachers paid attention to me due to my reading abilities and the foreignness they attributed it to rendered many friendships temporary or conditional. The dining table was once again a sanctuary, more than music or books since both required an ease with solitude at odds with my hunger for community. And it was always there, not everyone every time, but always someone, and music, food, and dialect that would remind me that America was not the world and that there were other ways of knowing and being in skin.

This is what carried me through high school and into college, and why I would eventually take classes in Black history and literature — boisterous old uncles in the family room during the World Cup with Red Stripe beer and aunties throughout the house, policing our pleasures and questioning our growth. Black strangers in the family comparing dialects and countries, and everyone lying about how beautiful, how sinless our national origins were. Trips to and from the airport and Western Union, mothball scent and newspaper wrapping.

Being Black was nothing if it was everything.

Maybe that was Aunt Joy or Aunt Pansy. Or maybe Uncle Tommy, who always claimed he was the happiest to be who he was when there were no others like him around. For him, Black Pride was an individual thing and had nothing to do with other Black people.

Songs we heard in the afternoon playing again in the dark. Graying heads over empty dishes, fighting to stay awake to forestall the inevitable return to that America outside. The young ones contemplating marijuana in the backyard, Cousin Brian lifting weights in the garage listening to Prince, Uncle Owen turning up the volume on Byron Lee and the Dragonaires. All of us around the dining table navigating Africa like planets orbiting the bright light of a long-dead sun.

Even now I don't know the details of Cousin Brian's crime or sentence. Even now I don't want to ask. Some say he was an accomplice, others say he pulled the trigger, and some say he wasn't even there. Others used to say more dramatic things: the more garish the crime, the more powerful his name would be when needed. I certainly couldn't ask his parents for details. They were in jail themselves, the house defined now by silence. Those few times they attempted to revive the dining table, the mood was sour, the arguments as unpalatable as the food now seemed. The guilt I felt was due to my part in those exaggerations of Cousin Brian's criminal prowess. In college, it was clear to me as an aspiring black scholar and writer how valuable it might be to have a relative in prison.

The phone call came in Aunt Pansy and Uncle Owen's house. We were at the dining table. My time spent at that house with them had become rare, which is why this event is easy to recall. My cousin had called from prison or maybe they had called him. I was unaware that such communication happened, and I realized that I might be the only one who wasn't talking to him regularly despite being the one who most often traded on his reputation. Even more surprising than the call itself was the fact that he asked to talk to me, the college boy who had already begun to learn what higher education meant for many black men—guilt and distance.

He asked how I was doing, if I was keeping my head up, if I was staying strong. He spoke faster than usual, as if our time was being measured, which, of course, it was. Maybe he spoke rapidly to prevent me from asking questions he couldn't or didn't want to answer. He'd heard that I was at university and congratulated me. I was embarrassed in the way I could be when admitting that I was in college to people in the neighborhood, especially those with impeccable street credentials. He was warm, sincere, and I wondered if prison had hardened his babyish face.

I was surprised when he said he wanted something from me.

Of course, I said, anything. Anything at all.

He wanted the newspaper published by the Black Student Association. He'd started reading in prison and had become radicalized. His focus was now on racism and oppression, and he'd heard much about the militancy of the Black Student Association and its newspaper. They'd had something to do with bringing the controversial leader of the Nation of Islam, Minister Louis Farrakhan, to campus and that had made news. I told him that I'd actually been at that talk and he was impressed.

Not only was I to get copies of the paper to him, I was to get the BSA to communicate directly and educate him on the issues facing oppressed black people in the white man's America. In fact, he wanted all the information I could send him, not only about America but on the whole diaspora.

I think he assumed I'd become king of my university.

Getting copies of the paper wasn't the problem. It was likely that all this would have done wonders for my reputation with the BSA, which, in fact, was the problem. Since arriving on campus, I'd been struggling to be a part of both the BSA and the African Student Association (the ASA). I was grateful there was as yet no Caribbean Student Association on campus.

As was the fashion on college campuses, the BSA had become Afrocentric. Radical students were no longer black but *African*, and the spelling wavered between the conventional spelling with a *c* or a more militant *k*. Yet this interest in Africa occurred alongside an open and casual prejudice toward Africans, including those in the ASA. There were BSA gatherings and meetings where Africans were described as dirty or having strong and unwelcome smells. They were described as being too dark and their lips and noses too big. The term "African booty scratcher" from my early days in America was revived.

Because some of the members of the BSA thought me Jamaican, not African, they spoke freely. When others caught themselves, they would then say things like "You're really one of us" or "We should be in solidarity against white oppression" as a way to escape responsibility for the insult. Africans were regularly seen as "not Black enough." This meant they were either not angry enough about racism or didn't understand it at all. But worse even than ideological or cultural differences was something more potent for a young man navigating this terrain: Africans were simply undateable.

The breaking point came when the newly radicalized BSA changed its name to the ASA, the *Afrikan* Student Association. They did it without conversation or concern. Blackness was theirs, after all. This posed a significant problem for the ASA, or what some took to calling the *African* African Student Association. The group was livid but essentially powerless. They were culturally and socially outgunned.

Unable to convey these details in a conversation both brief and likely monitored by the state, I told him yes. I would get him a copy of the paper. I would get him a full subscription. I would put him in touch with the editors and their prison outreach program if they had one, which if they didn't, they most surely should, and perhaps I should start one because so many brothers in prison were there due to the system of oppression that spread all the way from Africa through the Middle Passage and to the New World.

In other words, I did what I had become so good at. I lied.

9

Young Americans

My new job tutoring students for the college's affirmative action program was much better than scrubbing pots and serving food in a graduate dorm, which was how I'd contributed to my tuition payments up until then. It was also better than working for Great-Uncle Irving in his carpentry shop. Our relationship became more difficult for us both to tolerate the deeper I got into college. He may not have had a high school or college education, but he was smart enough to be certain that the ideas he heard me talking about were an absolute waste of time—and money, because I'm sure he occasionally helped my mother supplement my tuition. Most of the students I tutored were African American so the job delivered escape not only from Great-Uncle but also a way to render my political stance so clear that it wouldn't seem as if I were hiding from either of the two African student organizations, which I was.

The new job proved controversial at home. Great-Uncle Irving and other members of my family considered affirmative action a sign of intellectual laziness and a dependence on charity. We didn't need such things. People would assume me unworthy of my place at the university and assume we were scroungers.

Beyond this political push and pull, the affirmative action program shaped my political consciousness in a more intimate way: it was where I met the first person who would break my heart. She was African American, which was immensely significant. So was the fact that she was studying African history. I assumed her field of study was why she'd been open to dating me. She was the most beautiful woman I'd ever seen, so I was happy to exchange whatever Africanness I could still conjure for the relentlessly imagined pleasures that consumed me when I thought of her.

Tonight those pleasures would be realized. My mother was working very late or taking a night class as she often did. I'd cleared the living room and the bedroom so I wouldn't have to explain why the house had so much stuff everywhere. I'd installed cheap scented candles from a liquor store. But by the time we turned off the 10 freeway onto Crenshaw and the neighborhood took on its distinct shape and feel, my young lady's arms were crossed. I assumed she was nervous; many people who exited the freeway here got nervous. To make her feel comfortable, I pointed out places that mattered to me, where family members or friends lived or where you could get your hair braided for cheap or hear music on the weekends. I indicated a row of houses where Black fraternities lived and showed her the Jamaican restaurant that bore my mother's maiden name.

After a moody, withdrawn silence, she said, "I didn't realize you lived in the ghetto."

It took time to register what she was saying.

"I mean, this is the *ghetto*. You grew up in the *ghetto!*"

Maybe this was a simple mistake, I thought. One had to live here to understand the differences in streets, topography, and culture. The ghetto was, of course, over there, on the other side of Crenshaw Boulevard. It was south of Century or on the other side of Inglewood Park Cemetery. From the top of Slauson where we lived, you could see it spread out flat and wide with long swaying palm trees that reminded us all of the Caribbean and me of Cousin Cecil, who could shimmy up them in a flash. It was definitely up near Normandie and Vermont, and if you got so far as Hoover, then even God couldn't help you.

No, we didn't live in the ghetto. We were near it, moved through it, and had learned to respect it as one learns to respect an angry sea. We lived just close enough to breathe with its ebb and flow, hear its roar, and feel its spume.

After passing Great-Uncle Irving's church, which I showed her in hopes of getting us back on track, she said, "You're not really African at all. At least not really."

At first it seemed a compliment to my assimilation. I was eager to find something positive in her words. We were here for a reason, after all, and what I was—or what she thought I was—was crucial to its fulfillment.

When we were alone in my mother's house and the candles were lit, I made my first move, drawing her shea butter smell into my lungs. She recoiled. She said she felt that she'd been duped. She'd accepted my affection for nonblack things like the science fiction books I read and the music I listened to but that was because she assumed I didn't know the codes of Black America. That I so adored David Bowie had required much of her, but she figured I couldn't have known better since I was a foreigner. But for me to have grown up in what she—and admittedly most people in Los Angeles—called the ghetto meant that I should have known the rules. My way of speaking or presenting myself had to have been pretention. I'd hidden or perhaps rejected my true *ghetto* identity.

This difficult knot came when I was far from receptive to complex ideas, given my hopes for the evening and her smell deep in my lungs and my fingers aching for touch. But I knew I'd failed. Needless to say, we didn't have sex that evening — or ever.

Her rejection would have much to do with my now-changed relationship to the city I'd grown up in and something to do with my increased focus on more racially charged topics as I soon passed from undergraduate to graduate studies at the same school. That need to intellectually overcompensate for a failed racial identity or a general cultural alienation would be shared with many of the graduate students I began to know. So many of them were either immigrants themselves or rejects from cultures and communities that had bruised and still haunted them. A new community began to shape itself, one where our radicalisms were largely products of individual betrayals and personal failures. It became a home of sorts but then eventually, for many of us, careers.

I remember a T-shirt I'd see at reggae concerts, spoken-word events, hip-hop shows, or African culture festivals in the park near Great-Uncle Irving's house. It read MARCUS (as in Garvey), MALCOLM (as in X), MARTIN (as in Luther King), and ended with ME. They were sold all along Crenshaw Boulevard along with other clothes emblazoned with the colors, slogans, and images of Black radical politics. The message on the T-shirt suited the obsession with racial leadership that seemed necessary for social or professional advancement on campus. For example, these T-shirts had also become popular among members of the newly renamed Afrikan Student Association and other Black activist groups. Students wore these clothes, often with leather medallions embossed with images of Africa, and there were now drum circles in the quad and homemade incense burning everywhere. It was like when my mother and I had first arrived in Jamaica. Africa—or at least a version of it—was everywhere.

Students I knew who'd been prejudiced against African students and central to the usurping of the name African Student Association were suddenly transformed into oracles of the race, complete with dreadlocks and African names. But I now understood. These acts and performances were necessary given the pervasive doubt cast over our very presence on campus. We were assumed to owe our places there due to affirmative action. The more our qualifications were questioned, the more radical we Black students became. I convinced myself that whites did not discriminate between and among us, so racism was more important a problem than whatever internal wounds we caused one another, even heartbreak. Whatever traces of resentment I felt toward my fellow students I could chalk up to my cynicism and frustrated desire. And graduate school was like having your heart broken every week.

I cleared my shelves of science fiction and threw out Bowie and Prince and all the music they had led me to. I bought a few of those T-shirts from Crenshaw Boulevard, bales of incense from Black Muslim brothers on the corner, and took to traveling through the streets of the city attempting to put myself back together. With help from marijuana from the reggae shop next to the restaurant that bore my mother's maiden name and cheap alcohol from corner liquor stores, Los Angeles became the canvas for my reinvention, along with my classes, meetings with activist groups focused on everything from protesting racism to organizing rent parties and poetry readings, to the occasional drum circle. There was much to understand but even more to prove.

Still, no amount of Afrocentric or gangsta rap could hide the fact that in the weeks and months following the breakup I heard Bowie's "Young Americans" in my head whenever I thought about my young lady. And I thought about her often. That song had been a hit the year my mother and I had arrived in LA. Its lyrics referred to leaving Washington and the notion of the ghetto, but for obvious reasons, the chorus made me wince most of all: "She wants the young American, *all night!*"

When longing turned to anger, I recalled that my young lady

didn't even live in the neighborhood. Being African American gave her the authority to determine who was in or out of the racial community. Despite what she'd called the neighborhood, almost nobody who lived there or nearby used the word "ghetto" to describe it. Hip-hop, at least for our generation, was to blame for a new geographic elasticity around the word, which had become fashionable among many of the black students on campus. The location of "ghetto" expanded until it became larger than any map could hold yet so small that only they, the arbiters, could tell where its borders were.

I should have told my young lady that my family knew and understood poverty very, very well. In their eyes, what they were surrounded by in that part of Los Angeles was not that. In their countries, "ghetto" meant something else. It didn't mean hot and cold running water, a television in every or any room, fast food on every corner, free education, and regular electricity. As immigrants, they were also held hostage by an optimism fueled by those they'd left behind. Folks back home wanted only good news about America. Tales of racial suffering or economic disparity were seen as a case of those with wings to fly complaining about the thin air above.

I didn't tell her these things because they were too difficult to think or say at the time. The anger that gave rise to such thoughts now quickly turned back to longing, and I had started using the word "ghetto" like everybody else to emphasize the racism that I now agreed shaped and maintained the community.

My family was incensed to hear me refer to our neighborhood that way; they had long since tired of my tendency to explain everything by way of racism. For them, "ghetto" described a way of life, or rather the acceptance of that way of life. It was a synonym for choice, therefore it could be judged. There was nothing racial about it. Speaking perhaps for them all, Great-Uncle Irving once said to me over the dining table, "Boy, this racism is better than your daddy's genocide so shut up and keep breathing."

He stopped speaking to me for at least two years after that, which I welcomed. What I didn't welcome was Aunt Pansy's greeting me with the sadness of a funeral, especially when I began twisting my hair into dreadlocks. This was the price to pay for becoming Black, I thought. But because what I was becoming was actually American, I began to blame my parents and family for everything, especially for not understanding who or what I had become. They were immigrants after all, still fighting battles they had already lost back in their old countries.

I may have alienated my family, but I thrived on campus and in the broader neighborhood around Crenshaw and South Central, becoming a significant figure after participating in more protests and events than I could count. I published a Black student literary journal with funding from the English department and local Black businesses. People looked to me knowing that I had a gift for identifying racism in any situation or context and that I was always ready to speak out in classes and the neighborhoods. The universe was indeed black and white. I'd discovered the formula and was achieving my middle name, Voice of the People.

I joined the ASA (the *Black* one) even if it meant that the now-nameless African student group looked at me with suspicion. That didn't trouble me, since they all thought of me as Jamaican now, with my twisted-up hair and the accent they could never quite place. When the ASA gave me an award for my campus and community activism, it was my young lady who presented it to me. And when she hugged me on stage and her shea butter scent went immediately into my lungs, the clarity I'd found began to dissipate into what seemed like smoke rising from a near horizon.

I carried the award home and stared at it for hours, ignored it for days, then stared at it again for an entire weekend. It looked like glass but wasn't, and my name and achievements were stuck to it with plastic film. Eventually, I accepted that I deserved the award. Not for my achievements but for the depth and scale of my failures.

I welcomed the riots when they came. I wanted the entire country, or the parts of it that I'd struggled so much to fit into, to burn. As the violence spread, I made my way back to my mother's house from campus, staring down grim white faces in the opposing traffic. I spent the nights of smoke and fire and sirens drunk on cheap brandy and even cheaper marijuana. I walked the length of Crenshaw and sat in the park. The last time I saw my young lady was there, at an African pride festival, her pregnant belly festooned with cowrie shells, her hair wrapped in West African fabric, her feet stamping to rhythms churned out by Rastafarian drummers. On the streets during the riots, everyone was listening to rap on boom boxes and in cars, shouting out the lyrics and screaming, "Fuck the police!"

In my headphones was David Bowie's *Diamond Dogs.*

This ain't rock and roll, this is genocide.

I wished I had the courage to burn something without losing anything. And in the darkest hours, I wished I had nothing to lose.

After the riots, the petty grievances of campus life became harder to justify with inflated talk of the "struggle" or the "people." I was exhausted, hollowed out, reduced to ash. I wanted more than anything to be an immigrant again or at least go back to the beginning of the story that had brought me to this country, hopeful and naïve. I wanted to be African again.

10

Absolute Beginners (Part II)

Almost everyone in our family immediately blamed my mother's illness on her recent trip to Nigeria, the one that would be her last. This was especially true of Great-Uncle Irving, who hadn't wanted her to go at all. I suspect her refusal to blame Nigeria explained her reluctance to see a doctor until she was beyond the power of stubbornness. Of course, Nigeria had nothing to do with her cancer, but that didn't stop Great-Uncle Irving from believing she was being punished for her foolishness in returning to Africa.

After her diagnosis, conversations about the past became routine between my mother and me, urgent even. It wasn't just mortality that made her voluble, it had something to do with her discovery of gin and tonic late in life, especially with a drop of sweetened lime juice. I'd assumed her reluctance to share her history with me had something to do with shame or certainly trauma. But no, it was because she had assumed it would be easier for me to think of Africa in abstractions like most of my Black American friends and peers did. She chose not to upset my precarious new sense of belonging with confounding details of personal history.

Even more surprising than her desire to now talk about the past was that she encouraged me to write down what she was saying and at a certain point to even use a tape recorder. She spoke primarily about my father, godfather, Biafra, and sometimes, with prodding, England. Only after some time and after my perfecting the right combination of sweetened lime juice to gin and tonic did she become disoriented enough to accept herself as protagonist.

"I want to hear about 1963, when you arrived in Nigeria. That was when the country was still 'brimming,' as you used to say. Three years after independence, right, four years before the civil war. But first you should tell me how you met him."

"I told you this before. You should record it. Where is that small-small machine?"

"It's just not the same as writing down what you've said. I don't like writing what I hear back on it if that makes any sense."

It clearly didn't because she looked down and away, looking for her cat. I'd come to interpret this gesture as a polite way of indicating loss of interest. Then she'd wrinkle her brow as if trying to recall something important and fall asleep. Sometimes her eyes remained open and her mouth carried the suggestion of a smile, and sometimes her expression told me that the direction of our conversation was taking a great toll. Because she was taking so much medication, I never took those gestures personally.

"Each time you tell me something, it makes a different impression. I want to gather up all the different things that come up each time."

She must have wondered if my focus on creativity was in some way a refusal to properly engage the material spread throughout her home, stacked up against and covering surfaces, so when I did encounter the actual color of the walls, it came as some surprise. Also, she saw many of my questions as trivial, since only Biafra was of historical significance. That event eclipsed all that had come before it, including the story of Caribbean immigrants migrating to postwar England, the now-famous Windrush generation, named after the first ship that had brought them to the

"Mother Country" in 1948. She hadn't been on that boat but on one of the subsequent ones in 1952.

"How we met. I must have written it down somewhere in one of the letters or notes or something. As you always complain, I saved everything."

"Actually, I found his military diary the other day," I said.

The fabric that covered her head tilted to reveal her almost hairless scalp.

"His diary from Sandhurst?"

"Not from Sandhurst. It said FEDERATION OF NIGERIA, DIARY 1963, so it was before Biafra. His rank was captain then."

She made a weak smile and leaned back against the mountain of cushions she needed in order to sit up even for short periods of time.

"The very first thing I saw when I opened the diary at random was February 16, 1963, a Saturday."

I paused and watched to see if there would be a response. It was only visible to a mother's child.

"He wrote that he got engaged to you at Pat —"

"Ha, Pat Lake's house," she said. "Pat was one of my dear friends, an English girl."

"Then he said he danced with you."

"I was working in Bristol in those days. He was training all over the place. It was very rigorous — he and the other officers like your godfather were very serious. There are pictures here of them running and jumping and doing field exercises. You must have found them. For God's sake, all these African officers were getting their countries back! That was the excitement. But he never seemed tired. When your father showed up to see me, the little boy in the house told his parents that an African soldier was at the door."

"And so again, how did you meet him?"

"It was like *Doctor Zhivago*. Lovely film. And the music!" She began singing a song that I eventually discovered was called "Somewhere, My Love," or "Lara's Theme." "What I remember about that film was the love story and the revolution and trains. It was on a train where we first saw each other, you know. I don't remember if I was going to London from Bristol or from Bristol to London or somewhere else. I was with a friend, probably Pat Lake. We were walking to our seats, and there in front of me were these long legs stretched out across the aisle. I said, *Excuse me, please,* and the rest of his body appeared, in uniform. He and his friend were talking their language, and they acted like it was their private car. Nobody West Indian would have acted that way. I thought maybe he didn't speak English. But then he did the most extraordinary thing. He stood up and made his friend stand up too, both bowing."

Her wonderment was infectious.

"What did he say? What did you say?"

"Well, I still thought he didn't speak English. He just stared at us as I said thank you and we walked by. We found our seats in the next car."

"That's really all? You didn't look back or he didn't try to get your attention?"

"Girls like us didn't *look back*. And to West Indian people, that was just beyond the pale — Africans. I knew some people moved with them in London, but those were islanders from a lower class, people we would have called bush people back in Jamaica."

"I know there was some hostility to the marriage from the Jamaican side."

"From my English friends too, but for a different reason. They thought it wouldn't be safe to go where people lived in trees and such foolishness. But my English friends relaxed when they saw him in his uniform and heard his English and found out about Sandhurst. There was some glamour there, like some of the Africans who were going to Oxford and Cambridge, or the ones we saw on telly after Ghana was independent. Dark glasses, and speaking English very properly."

"Ghana's independence was 1957."

"We thought of it as the first black one and so in London it was quite a thing."

She began to sing a calypso. I recognized it as the legendary calypsonian Lord Kitchener's "Birth of Ghana."

Smiling, eyes closed, swaying as much as she could, she continued. "I think that might be when we began to really notice the Africans. All the race riots and things were going on in London, and then suddenly it was all about Ghana and then Nigeria, Guinea, Cameroon. The Black Man was on the rise, Africa this and that and other such things. But I tried not to get all caught up in that at first. I was there for a reason."

"Sounds like quite a time to be in England."

"Well, I was in Bristol, which was not a quiet place, mind you. But it did seem that black people in England were all abuzz, and there was Cuba too and Kenya, and Egypt. Independence everywhere and all over the place! At first, I didn't pay much attention because I was working and studying and sending money back home. I made it to staff nurse and was a midwife. Suddenly, white people had black nurses who were delivering white babies and tending to the dying. People were not happy and there is no anger like the anger that comes when people have no choice in the matter. But we were professionals. We were supposed to be cultural ambassadors and I still think we were even though your generation doesn't believe that. I didn't know any Africans at all. It was only after I met him that I realized how close I'd been to them the whole time. I mean they had been there all along! Not knowing them couldn't have been an accident."

"And he just shows up at your door in Bristol."

"Pat and I had on our nurses' uniforms, so that was it, you know, on the train. He asked around. He was famous for his charm. A prince among men, they said — really, they all said that. It's easy to be charming when you are tall. That's what Pansy said. Ha, he just knocked on the door in his uniform, standing tall, and the young boy of the house — a real rascal, far too curious for his own good, used to follow me around with the strangest questions, even asked to see my tail when I first arrived because so many English people thought we had tails! He came running back to the parlor where I was and said there was an African soldier at the door. Who would an African soldier be there to see?"

"And then six weeks later you were in Nigeria."

"But we were legally married in England or else it wouldn't have been right for me to go, of course, and then we had a grand state ceremony in Lagos."

"But six weeks!"

Of the photos she kept of my father, only two were of him without his uniform. In one he wore a dashiki and it softened his features and expression. His skin was pale as if washed out by the light from behind the camera. There had never been any talk of European or even Arabic/Fulani blood in our family, and in the other picture of him out of uniform—the only one of him and his family—his father and mother were as dark as all of the others.

"There was also a wedding announcement in his diary from Jamaica."

"I didn't save that, did I? My goodness. Well, at least you have more than you need. My parents, I suppose they couldn't resist, since I was getting married to an African prince. That was probably my fault. It was the only way to make them feel it was okay, to say he was a prince or a king, which wasn't true but not a lie either. Plus, I'm sure him having light skin made a positive impact on them. The pictures I sent them were of raised swords, uniforms, big cars; they had to have been proud. It was like proper English royalty but African."

"And that worked, you think?"

"For some, but the letters from home never stopped asking if he had other wives or about wild animals or things like that or if we lived in trees. But when the war started, they were just trying to find us. When we returned to Jamaica, they were just so happy to see me and my baby the son of an African king." She smiled.

"I don't remember much princely treatment in Jamaica."

"But you always exaggerate your suffering and how long it lasted. That's very American. Those people were good to you."

"Or maybe you diminish and try to forget the suffering. That's very English."

She looked away again, this time so emphatically that when the cat returned it seemed to do so to save us from the awkwardness.

I'd given up using the tape recorder during our sessions not only because the amount of material was so vast that it would be a challenge to transcribe but also because I realized that my mother could no longer fill the gaps in her story. This could only be done by making my own trip to Nigeria. She said as much, encouraging me to track down my godfather and talk to my uncles instead of trusting all the Biafra books that were still appearing. Until then, there was the gin and tonic and — in the wake of chemotherapy and a bone marrow transplant — occasional marijuana tablets.

"What was Lagos like when you arrived?"

"Someone said it was feeling itself be a city for the first time. It was probably Chris the poet who said that. Please make sure you write about Chris Okigbo. He was a dear, dear friend."

Her eyes went warm, almost tearing up. Because she seemed so hurt by her mention of Okigbo, I didn't tell her that everyone wrote about him now and that his death had attained far greater meaning than it had even in her time.

"But it was still colonial, still orderly and clean. There was pride in maintaining what the English left. That's gone now, I know. Most of my social life was in the officers' quarters, and we had house boys and house girls. A lot of dust and dirt, though."

"It looks amazing in the photos."

"It was! Even when people said that the Northerners were jealous of what we were doing in Lagos and the Muslims thought Igbos were corrupt and loving life too much, none of that mattered. Until they started killing us like diseased cattle, we thought that in Lagos there was room for everybody. But we were only thinking about Lagos."

"Cities that big can seem infinite."

"For most of the people, Lagos was replacing villages. There everyone was coming from everywhere. People from the villages were becoming Nigerian for the first time. A lot of our set were international, schooled in America, England, in Europe—not just military, but doctors, barristers, professors, and poets, and people from Ghana and Congo. And there was the civil-service set. Some of them were West Indian from before independence. Lagos wasn't as big as it is now, but there always seemed room. It was like America that way."

"So, you were in Lagos when people started moving east to Igboland."

"To Biafra. No, I was between Enugu, where you were born, and Onitsha. He was stationed there. You were born at the start of the bombing of the East. We traveled to Onitsha, where I was training nurses and midwives. We'd drive to Lagos for parties and visits. And when he went to the Congo with your godfather—"

"And that was for?"

"A United Nations mission after Patrice Lumumba was killed. While he was gone, I stayed in our village."

"You mention his traveling. He went to India too, right?"

"Yes, for a military training course. It was 1966."

"There was a coup that year that people say made the civil war happen."

She became withdrawn, and I wondered if it was the medication, the remembering, or both. The 1966 coup was a particularly bloody one, led by a cadre of soldiers who killed almost two dozen high-ranking political and social figures, including Nigerian Prime Minister Abubakar Tafawa Balewa and the Muslim leader of the North, Sir Ahmadu Bello, the Sardauna of Sokoto. This coup, led largely by Igbo leaders, was viciously subdued by the government, but it triggered a countercoup six months later by Muslim officers in northern Nigeria. Although the Igbo soldiers who had led the prior coup argued that its focus was anticorruption, the Muslim officers saw it as based on ethnicity. The countercoup caused a suspension of the Nigerian constitution. A military government was installed with Lieutenant Colonel Yakubu Gowon—my father and godfather's colleague from

Sandhurst—at its head. This installation justified in the minds of many Northerners a long-standing suspicion that Igbos were trying to take over the country. The cultural impact of Igbos—they were the first to embrace Christianity, the English language, and Western education—and their having a culture devoted to enterprise is why many described them as the "Jews of Africa." Their being targeted for genocide would seal that description.

"There is something that seems to obsess historians and doesn't make much sense to me," I said. "A lot of people say my father was a part of the 1966 coup, that he was their 'man in the East.' Why was he mysteriously sent to India just before it happened?"

"He went on a training course, yes, to India. He brought me that wooden egg I've shown you. You really liked playing with it when you were young but I kept it from you. You would have lost it. Do you know where it is?"

"But was he a part of that group that some think actually started the war? It seems to me that if he were going to lead a military strike he'd not suddenly leave right before to go to India."

"Could you bring me the egg, please? Look for it."

"And if he was involved, wouldn't he be arrested when he got back?"

"I will be truly distraught if that egg is not in this house."

"Okay then, let's talk about the village. Sometimes you stayed there alone."

"Boy, you know that you can never be alone in Africa." She laughed. "We used to say that all the time."

"But you were there alone after he died."

"Where else would I go? We came back to the village and stayed there until we left the country weeks before Biafra fell in 1970."

"I want to talk about that, but first I want to know what the village was like in the early days for you."

"Well, at first I did miss Lagos. But you know, the point was to become an Igbo wife. Even though your father always told me to be a Jamaica woman, God bless him. He and your godfather wanted the women in the village to be like me. Can you imagine? They imitate me while I was imitating them. Your godfather said I was the modern black woman, which I don't think meant anything to people in the village. He was very serious about Biafra being a symbol of the struggle of the Black Man, which I didn't understand at all."

"Why didn't you understand it?"

"Well, when we said it in England, we were talking about whites or racism or the color bar and all that. Here the Northerners and the federal government were also the Black Man, so what he said made no sense unless black was his way of saying something else; in which case, he should have found a better word."

Apparently, she'd accepted the logic of the Black Man only up to a certain point. It was a thing that men said. Such thinking became unacceptable when the federal government's blockade of Biafra started to produce lethal results. Britain was still her Mother Country despite the racism she'd encountered there, but it was aware of the starvation and violence in Biafra and discouraged other nations from intervening. With the numbers of people dying all around her as Biafra was brought to heel, it was clear that there was no more hope to be placed in the Mother Country or the Black Man.

"Maybe he meant that all Nigerians were struggling against the legacy of the British and colonialism. They were involved in this too."

"Ha, I think the British wanted the oil. They supported genocide to protect it. The worst thing to happen to Nigeria is they found oil in the East before independence. Our mistake was to think it would be without consequences."

"And that's still the main problem, the oil—"

"No, it's not the oil that's the main problem."

"Well, the British wanted it. I'm sure the Americans wanted it too. That's what I mean."

"That's not what you mean. I know what you mean."

"What do I mean?"

"You want to blame whites. You want to blame America. For everything."

This time I was the one who looked away. She was sitting

up now without the cushions. Her cat was in her arms, and she stroked it with great concentration. As revenge, I imagined her as the type of comic-book villain the Phantom or James Bond used to face who had cats to signify just how sinister they were.

When she talked about Biafra, she usually emphasized the oil and the fact that the British had supported the Nigerian Federal Government against Biafra due to it. This sudden refusal to see the war as colonial and racial was as much a comment on my god-father's faith in the Black Man as it was a critique of my own ra-cialized politics, which to her must have seemed similar.

It was, understandably, difficult to challenge her on these top-ics. She had seen men and boys in fragments, bones exposed and limbs held together by stretched skin. House boys and gardeners, teachers and merchants, priests and taxi drivers, friends and en-emies dying in ways that suggested depths of hatred that could not be explained by oil or borders or skin or arbitrary names like Nigeria or Biafra.

Then there was kwashiorkor, which haunted her for the rest of her life. She watched the bellies of children swell and their heads balloon, their bones fragile like long bits of coral found on Jamai-can beaches. In her view, it was indecent to assign blame for the violence itself. Nobody was "behind" all this. There were simply those who did the killing and those who did not, those who did nothing and those who did everything they could.

What surprised me was that her disillusionment with political explanations for genocide occurred after my father's death, not alongside it. But with so many dying every day and so many depending on her to manage their losses, she thought it selfish to give in to grief. There was no time to parse whatever ideologies may have contributed to the conflict. Then there was her child, me, not just a fatherless infant but now the head of a family, the first son of the first son. As such, I was less hers than her husband's family's. She would be shocked to discover her rights to the child were effectively annulled by her husband's death.

This part of the story, along with how my father actually died, had always been beyond her capacity to tell. There was nothing about it in her papers. It required information and insights that could only come from my own trip to Nigeria.

And what I would learn there was this: my father died near Onitsha, lungs pierced by shrapnel. Because this area never been shelled before, his men assumed that his location had been betrayed. That is why rumors of assassination always emerged when I asked my uncles or ex-soldiers about his death. Because my mother's new culture dictated that she marry her husband's brother, a ceremony was prepared within weeks of the funeral, and in the midst of war, rituals began. She, however, decided to run. I don't know if it was a moment of panic or a detailed plan. I also don't know how far she traveled before the family realized she was gone. What is known is that she wrapped her child in fabrics and drove as fast as she could across shelled-out roads and targeted fields past where her husband had been wounded to where she knew my godfather to be. Legend has it that upon discovering that the child had been taken — kidnapped, they say — her husband's mother had a heart attack and died on the spot.

My godfather arranged for her and her baby to board one of the airlifts that had been smuggling food and medical supplies into Biafra. We were bundled on a plane decades past its use and piloted by European mercenaries that was filled with starving children with only my mother to care for them. It may have been the last one that flew out before the secessionist nation collapsed, but that too could be legend.

The death of the first son, the loss of his son, and the death of the matriarch was enough to generate resentments that endured a long time. I realized why she had never sent me back to Nigeria until I had reached legal age and acquired American citizenship. She feared the family would keep me. She also feared that the families of notable figures of the secession and intimates of my godfather were likely to be persecuted after the war. From Gabon, though, she sent the family medicine, money, and items they could sell in the streets and markets. She started doing this when she made her way out of the refugee camp and found friends and supporters of my godfather's in Libreville, the nation's capital.

The things and money she sent kept the family alive when there was almost nothing left of Igboland.

I understand why it was difficult for her to see the war in purely abstract terms. When our conversations became a debate about blame or responsibility, when I spoke of racism or colonialism and she of the unfathomability of the violence, we both learned to end them. We eventually began to anticipate this pattern as the condition of a new kind of intimacy. It provided the shape of the story of mother and son, Africa and diaspora, America and a country left gutted to bleed out into a world.

She was asleep again, slumped against my shoulder. Not wanting to disturb her with my movements, I sat quiet and still, as I did sometimes for hours.

11

African Night Flight

My name was in my ears as I rushed across red dirt to the nearest tree and evacuated my stomach into a bright patch of green.

"Onuorah, are you okay?"

This bout of vomiting was painful. I hoped it would be the last even though I knew that this was unlikely. It could have been the stew served in my honor the night before when I had arrived in my ancestral village in Onitsha, the well-known city on the banks of the Niger River in Nigeria. The stew was made of the large river snails I'd seen hanging from strings on the edges of the central market. Or it could have been the stew earlier in the day made from local *ogbono* seeds. Likely, though, it was the alcohol. All rituals here seemed to involve heavy drinking. As I was the returned prodigal, saying no wasn't an option. But despite hangovers and vomiting, the alcohol served a useful purpose. It kept my emotions at bay, held me in check in the midst of a chaos of sensations and information.

"Your father was a good drinker, so you will be okay. You are just like him, I am sure of that. In the morning, your aunties will make you food my brother liked. He liked English food for breakfast, eggs and bacon, things like that, and we have bought them for you. Here you are the first son of the first son and can have anything you want."

These items must have been difficult for the family to procure, but the thought of Western food filled me with relief. From the moment I had disembarked in Lagos before traveling east to Onitsha, I'd rejected Western food. I intended to be seen as a native no matter how painful the process proved to be and regardless of how many uncles or cousins dared me to eat things so extreme that I came to relish the act of vomiting into gutters large enough to swallow children.

My uncle was a local politician and a renowned drinker. His taking me through the town at night involved not only copious amounts of alcohol but also sporadic welcome rituals with the sacred cola nut — the center of Igbo culture — and plates of mysterious, grilled bushmeat. Perhaps it was the bushmeat that finally turned my stomach. Also unsettling was the fact that whenever we were recognized I heard "The first son of the first son" or "Your father was a great man. You are him returned. Biafra is not dead."

"You hear that?" Uncle would say then. "This is where you are from. You are not like those Blacks over there who don't know where they are from and are always looking for roots and making noise about it. This is your home. You can trace where you belong right back to this place and can stop looking beyond."

He'd greeted me at the airport dressed in native finery and surrounded by a dozen men and women shuffling and dancing in traditional welcome. I assumed it was a tourist performance or something planned for a local dignitary. When it turned out to be for me, I knew in a terrifying moment that these were celebrations not of me but of their own expectations of me. I knew already that I would be unable to satisfy them.

There seemed no time or space for my own questions about my father or about my godfather or Biafra. There was no interest in such things. Only the material future mattered. The sudden pressure for me to conform to my family's desires was enough to render me almost catatonic, and I migrated through my homecoming barely able to ask substantive questions about my history.

Back in Lagos, all the talk had been about my returning to work in a bank or get into politics simply by attaching my name to my uncle's campaign or anyone else's or to work for an oil company, which was the real prize. It was also clear that my return to Nigeria would enable members of the family with political and business ambitions to get close to my godfather. A few months before I'd arrived for this visit, he'd returned from a twelve-year exile in the Ivory Coast. But because Igbos still thought of him as their rightful leader and referred to him as Eze Nd'Igbo, King of All Igbos, the federal government had put him under house arrest.

This evening, my uncle was whizzing me over irregular dirt roads at such speeds that there was no noticeable difference in the motion of his battered jeep whether he was drunk or sober. Everywhere we stopped, there was a cola nut broken in blessing followed by beer and "hot drinks," meaning spirits.

I remember meeting someone with a grand title who was dressed in white. My uncle fell to his knees and prostrated himself before the man. He asked me to do the same, and when I did, everyone laughed, including the man dressed in white. Apparently, there were ways of bowing that I did not know. Another time I was asked to give a toast to a group of old men under a large tree and speak on behalf of my family. Some complained that I didn't speak Igbo. Others argued that although it was true that I'd left the country too young to learn the language I could still learn when I returned for good. This didn't placate those who'd complained, but after a few more rounds of drink, anything I said drew cheers. All I needed to do was keep suggesting that I would soon be coming home to repair whatever rifts in their lives they still traced back to Biafra. And pay for drinks.

Then at some point in the dark, we were in a house full of women sitting on cushions and listening to local music. They smiled hospitably while I waited for my uncle to return from wherever he'd gone. The house boy brought more beer, easy to drink due to the incredible heat and lack of clean water. The women ranged in age and girth, some in heavy makeup, some in traditional clothing, and others in Western dress. A large older woman came into the room and sat with me. She was clearly the owner of this place, and I could smell the mix of sweat and perfume.

"You are the American nephew. They say your father was famous from the war."

I nodded.

"I want to go to America one day. I think I should be there. Don't you think?"

I was too drunk to follow my ideological instinct, which was to tell her about racism and capitalism, but not too drunk to remember where I was. Telling these people these things would be a sign of how much of a native I wasn't.

"You will help me get there, okay? You will send invitation letter and then ticket."

This had been asked of me many times since I'd arrived in Nigeria, and I never knew how to respond. Eventually, I realized that I didn't need to respond since it was never really a question but a claim. Everything was settled because they'd asked and I was the American through whom all things were possible.

She reached into her bosom and pulled out a small piece of paper. On it was her name and her mailing address.

I took the paper.

"Hey! America," she squealed at the other women who looked at her jealously. "America! I'm going to be American! I will come and go as I please!"

She got up and restructured the fabric wrapped around her generous waist and hips. One of the younger women came over to me and took my hand.

I followed her into a smaller room that had a bed we sat on.

"It's okay," she said. "Don't worry. I am clean. I have a doctor." She pulled from her pocket some kind of card as proof. With red dirt stains everywhere and my breath reeking of vomit, I feared the outcomes of this particular ritual. But I did appreciate the privacy so I lay down on the bed.

"Are you sure you are okay?" she asked.

"Yes, I'm okay, but all I want is to lie here."

She laughed. "What will I tell your uncle?"

"What do you mean?" I sat up.

"Your uncle. Don't you know why he brought you here?"

"Yes, of course."

"Ha, it's not just that. He wants to make sure you like women."

I was too drunk to be angry. The expression on my face made her laugh.

"Don't worry," she said. "I never met a Black American. I will say the right thing."

When we went out into the main room, my uncle was waiting, his arm around the woman who had given me her address.

"Is it okay?" he asked. I nodded, but then he took the young woman into a corner and began speaking to her in Igbo. I watched her smile and nod her head enthusiastically. He looked over at me with a massive grin.

Somewhere later and somewhere else, someone was baking bread, or at least it smelled like it. The people around me were different but the same, or at least they were saying the same things. I was saying the same things too; they only seemed different due to the level of inebriation I'd achieved. I was praying for dawn when I'd be with the young cousins who did not drink and my aunties who had less complicated expectations than my uncles. When I awoke, I was quickly helped into my uncle's jeep. My uncle was helped in also, put in the driver's seat, his hands placed on the wheel. I don't know how long we sat there, but we eventually began lurching forward and then stopping, moving in bursts. The jeep had bent the gate of someone's compound, just barely missing the gutter that was wide enough to sink a portion of the vehicle. The gateman came out cursing until he recognized my uncle and receded into the darkness.

We reached our family compound sometime near dawn. Uncle almost had to crawl into his house, the central building, which I'd been told my father had built before the war for his new bride, my mother. I was staying in a house farther in back, and to reach it, I had to pass my father's grave. There was no headstone because where he was actually buried was only approximate. At that time during the war, everything was chaos and the family temporarily had to abandon the compound. Because there had been no ceremony my father wasn't officially dead. According to tradition he was still alive, waiting for me to bury him.

The only good thing about being this drunk, I thought, was that it would be easy to sleep in the brutal subtropical heat. Even the mosquitos couldn't keep me awake now. But too soon it was morning, and the promised eggs, bacon, and toast were there. Also, blessedly, there was powdered coffee.

But then I was on the road again, this time on foot with a group of young cousins. We walked the pocked and jagged red-dirt roads through a staggering sprawl of structures that seemed to have been arranged by rolling a handful of dice and building wherever one landed. There were houses, sheds, and a few bars, restaurants, and garages, sometimes all three in the same building, brick mostly, some rising up four or five floors. Nothing escaped the red dust. New things seemed heavy with time.

One young cousin said, "Big Brother, you have to get rich very soon. Not just for us but your mum. Uncle says you should build a school or hospital here in her name because she saved so many people and children. People remember your dad but many remember your mum."

The size of my hangover made me agreeable, and the humidity rendered me helpless in the face of his relentless talking.

"When you come back, you can get a job with accounts. You can travel and shop in the UK, and if you get sick or your family, you can go there. That's the way it is here and you can have it. With your father's name, you can even do politics. In the East, people will vote just when they hear that name."

"Yes, Big Brother," said another cousin. "Here it doesn't matter what you studied over there, just that you have the degree. With your godfather, you can do anything."

I'd given up tracing actual relationships given how many cousins, uncles, and aunties emerged from seemingly everywhere upon my arrival.

A record shop was blasting rap music. My cousin got excited.

"Big Brother, Big Brother, let me sing a music for you!"

He was a dark boy, stretched tall and with an impressive natural Afro. I'd thought he was Yoruba, not Igbo.

"Listen, Big Brother." He stopped us all in the road and began rapping.

"It doesn't matter if the cat is black or white; it's how he catch the mouse!"

His eyes were so open with pride that they seemed unnatural. He repeated his lyrics just in case I didn't understand their cleverness and gravity.

"It doesn't matter if the cat is black or white if it's catching the mouse! You see?"

"Yes, I understand, but what do you mean by it?" I wanted to know how issues of race and racism translated here. But I was pretty sure this cousin had never ever seen an actual white person. There were very, very few this far east.

"It means that the cat can be any color if it can catch the mouse."

"I understand, but what are you saying about race? That it doesn't matter at all?"

He was perplexed. "Big Brother, there are cats of many color who can catch mouse the same way and that is a good thing. That is my music."

"Yes, but you are rapping about skin color and black and white people."

He was stunned now, his eyes even bigger than before.

"Big Brother, no, I don't know about this black or white people thing. That is not what my song is saying. I'm talking about the cats and why the color of them is not what matters but the catching of the mouse. Do you get?"

I worked hard to suppress a chuckle. He had been talking about cats after all. My chuckle escaped. Thank goodness it was seen by him as sudden comprehension.

Cousins joined us and disappeared as we got closer and farther from the areas where they lived. I began to assume that the best way to evaluate the strength of kinship was by proximity to our compound.

From three or four days of walking or being driven around by my uncles, I came to recognize particular areas by the shore of the great murky river or near the central market. These places seemed distinguishable only by virtue of their relationship to our family. Belonging here meant being attached to territory marked by those who bore a particular name for centuries. It made sense then to imagine my very blood stained by all this red dust.

Or perhaps belonging meant turning up yet another indistinguishable road miles into another labyrinthine village and encountering someone screaming at the top of aged lungs, "Onuo-raegbunam! Sokei. Sokei. Onuoraegbunam!"

I spotted an old woman with gnarled skin and a thin white beard leaning out a window. I recognized my last name, but she'd said my middle name in a way I'd never heard it.

"Big Brother, we must greet her. She knew your dad and your mum."

That she'd known my parents was unsurprising, so many I met had, but that she knew this stranger, me, was shocking. She'd seen us coming up the road and immediately began calling out my name. She came out to the road and fell to her knees, holding my hand to her face.

"Onuoraegbunam! Sokei, *nno. Nno, O? Nno! Chukwu d'aalu, Chukwu d'aalu!*"

She began bobbing her shoulders and dancing despite her limited mobility. She didn't speak English, but I knew that *nno* meant "welcome"; *Chukwu*, of course, meant "God"; and *d'aalu* meant "give thanks" or "thank you." But why did she call me Onuo-raegbunam? What was that last part added on to my middle name?

"It's your name," said one of my cousins. "That's your name."

"My middle name is Onuorah."

"That's your name too. The whole of it."

After the old woman danced and embraced me and then returned to her window, I asked my cousins what "egbunam" meant. None of them knew. I assumed it was because for many of them Igbo was no longer a first language. Even if they were fluent in it, some names and terms were hazy or archaic.

When we returned to the compound later that afternoon, my youngest uncle, a barrister, was there.

"Oni, are you home?"

"Yes, Uncle. From walking the village and town."

"God is great," he said. "This is wonderful. How was it? Did you enjoy yourself after your busy night?" There was a sly smile there, but I couldn't tell just how sly it was meant to be. As I said, he was a barrister.

"I'm still very tired."

"Ha, yes, many people want to see you. It will be my turn to take you around this night so take some sleep." He called the house boy and told him to take a cold beer to my room. "That will help you."

"Thank you. Uncle, I met an old woman today. She saw me out of a window and called out to me. She recognized me."

"Which woman? What was her name?"

"I don't know, but she was very old and was very happy to see me."

"Everyone is happy. Very happy. God is great. Not everybody comes back."

"But she called me a different name, or a different version of my name."

"Really? What did she call you?"

"I won't pronounce it correctly, but she called me Onuoraeg-bunam."

"Yes, that is your name. From your father."

"But my name is Onuorah."

"No, Oni, it is Onuoraegbunam. Your full name. You don't know your name?"

"My mother, well, since I was a child it was Onuorah. 'Voice of the People.'"

"That is only the first part. This is the second part of it, the complete name."

I felt as if I were sobering up, or at least my head seemed to allow greater clarity due to a rush of adrenaline.

"What does the second part mean?" I asked him.

"Onuorah is 'Voice of the People,' but egbunam means . . . well, something like 'Will Always Be Against Me' or 'What People Say Will Not Stop Me, or, Won't Kill Me.'"

"So, my name is the Voice of the People Will Always Be Against Me?"

"Well, maybe, something like that. It means a controversial person. Your dear mum, her Igbo was never too good but she tried, oh, she tried . . . God is great."

He left me standing amid a swirl of mosquitos. I began think-ing, remembering. My name, my names. It wasn't just the alcohol or even the antimalaria tablets, which brought dreams more vivid than the ones I had when hospitalized in Jamaica.

On my way back to my room, I stopped by my father's grave. All I could do was stare at it and wonder: How did he know? How did my father know my name?

Despite my godfather being under house arrest in Lagos and regu-larly blamed by the federal government for the deaths of millions, photos of him and his wife were everywhere, particularly on the covers of the fashion and lifestyle magazines hawked by sweat-soaked boys in traffic. She was a lawyer, but what had caught the public's attention was that she was some three decades his junior and had represented the country in the Miss Universe contest. To add to the scandal, my godfather was rumored to have been her godfather too, and her father disowned her on hearing of the re-lationship. The king of a people who famously had no kings was now the prince of the tabloids. A visitor from outer space would have assumed that he was the president or an avuncular pop star.

He'd insisted on seeing me. I prepared to navigate the paparazzi clustered around his compound and the political wannabes within. My time in the village had exhausted me. I'd settled into a numbness indistinguishable from an extended hangover. I had absorbed too much history in too short a time. America, oddly, was where I knew these experiences in Nigeria would make sense.

My mind was swirling with memories of the village and nonstop impressions of Lagos, the scale and size and relentless motion rendering thoughts of the past — thought itself — irrelevant. I would later regret this because I simply couldn't ask my godfather most of the questions I'd prepared. I could barely even speak. Luckily, he was like most Biafra veterans I'd met, eager to talk about my father. Unlike the others, though, he wasn't interested in telling me how much I paled in comparison. I managed to tell him how difficult it was to get real, human details about my father. Everything was myth, romance, *Doctor Zhivago*. What was he really like? I'd been imagining my father as the ultimate man of his time, an über Igbo, as it were.

"Oh no," said my godfather. "He was always quite different." And it was probably there that I began using "quite" in his quite British way. "I think that's why he married your mother, really. She wasn't like anything he'd known or seen. That woman has such *power!* You should have seen her during the bombings and carrying you around on her back while tending to our men and boys and setting up clinics. I remember when he told me about her at Sandhurst. He never mentioned she was Jamaican so I just thought he'd found some Churchillian English woman with a straight back and thick ankles. I mean, quite a few of us were marrying English in those days. It was difficult to avoid, you see. But a Jamaican? That, my boy, was a curious angle of approach. *Very* curious."

He burst out laughing, a rich chuckle that brought his chin close to his chest and made his eyes look up at me mischievously.

"Will you take another beer? Star or Gulder or perhaps a stout?"

I told him I preferred Gulder to Star or stout. He was happy that I knew my Nigerian beers. It was a sign of something good, of a certain kind of man.

"He was an Onitsha man, but Onitsha people have always been different. You know we Igbos are called the Jews of Africa? Onitsha people are the most Jew-like, if you will. But he was different among the different. No matter how wild his deviations, everyone assumed them appropriate. Everything he did was accepted as traditional, even marrying your mother. If he did something, it was Igbo. Simple. That's why he was the *new* Onitsha man. Those two were really the JFK and Jackie O of Biafra. You've heard that before?"

"Yes, I've heard it before."

"They were modern, what we should have been."

"What was it that made him different among the different, as you say? He must have been aware of that, and it must have made him, I don't know, self-conscious, maybe a little alienated? Maybe that's what drew him to my mum."

"He knew she was the woman he should—not would, mind you, *should*—marry. He didn't know anything about her other than she wasn't English or African even though they were both British as we all were then. We weren't American yet." He began to laugh.

He trailed off and began to search the ceiling for the precise words. He found them above a small window in the far corner next to an enormous portrait of his wife.

"Alienation, cultural confusion, those things I know are great concerns these days. I've read the books. But truly they were foreign to us. We were not racked with doubt. We'd been colonized, but we were not confused. Or we wouldn't have fought at all! Perhaps you could say that things were clearer then. It's a sad thing that those things matter so much now. I wonder if it's really regret, not ours but of those who write about us. Because we had none."

I thought to ask if he really had no regrets about Biafra, the secession, genocide, and the horrible disease of hunger. Could one lose or even win a war without regrets? But I didn't want to sound like a journalist or an academic or yet another historian trying to get the truth from the great man. I suspected that a man like him dared not succumb to regret. It would have been to finally and truly lose the war.

We had dinner alone, mostly in silence until a house boy appeared with an ex-soldier who unveiled a television at the other end of the room. More beers arrived. The TV screen lit up with white noise. I was surprised when the house boy immediately turned it to American professional wrestling, but I was stunned when my godfather erupted with joy.

"Wonderful," he said. "You must pay attention to this."

"You enjoy wrestling?" I asked, my surprise likely tinged with some scorn.

"Don't you?" I think he noted that scorn. "You don't have to agree with it to enjoy it, you know."

As I was at the high point of my ideological period, his latter statement was hard to process. I wasn't yet able to enjoy and disagree with anything at the same time. But the idea that I was watching American wrestling with an infamous warlord was almost too much to process.

"The pageantry," he said, "it is committed to rituals."

"But you know it's fake, right?" I asked.

He didn't seem troubled by my assertion, just curious about it.

"I mean the whole thing is staged, and it's so unreal, the violence."

"But what's unreal about that?" he asked.

"It's all set up, predetermined."

"Violence is always quite unreal even if you prepare for it. And warfare is not without its manipulations. If things go well, they should seem predetermined."

At this point I began to wonder if there was a lesson in this, answers to questions I had been failing to ask. Or was this just a meandering conversation between an old man and his hungover godson?

"But I see. It disappoints you," he said.

"Well, yes, the fact that it is or could be fake loses something."

He paused but continued looking at the screen. Then he turned back to me with a look of great compassion.

"But hasn't it become more interesting to you because it could be false? Isn't that an added pleasure?"

I began to laugh. Was this the lesson?

"So you should be as invested in *not* knowing as I am," he said.

"Why?"

"Well, your pleasure comes from doubting. Mine comes from believing, and we should assume that our pleasures are of the same quality or we would be barbarians."

I laughed out loud. Was this the lesson?

Just then someone pulled off an impressive and surprising move. A body doubled over in midair. The canvas shook and the audience erupted. There may have been a splash of blood or the suggestion of limbs overextended.

"You see," said my godfather. "It is real enough."

Then it was full night and the generator was on, meaning the electricity had gone. The television was off, and my godfather's wife arrived quietly. Before I left the house, he disappeared for a time, leaving me sitting with her. She was not called the most beautiful woman in Nigeria for nothing. When he returned, she said she was stunned that I had even come back to Nigeria at all, given that Biafra had sent me so far away for so long. I had earned an enviable right — the right to forget Nigeria completely. I had truly and completely become something else. I half expected her to say that I'd become an American. Even though that would have been true, she didn't say it and my love for her became permanent.

But my godfather disagreed with her reading of things. He said the fact that I did return and would continue to return was proof of belonging. The taking up of obligations, however painful, however absurd, was confirmation of a choice being made. It was greater than blood or habit. Belonging, he said, had nothing to do with being accepted. It was about duty.

He gave me a letter addressed to my mother.

"When you return to Nigeria for good, there will be much more for us to talk about. I have great plans for the future. You must be a part of them."

* * *

The letter was in my hand, moist with night sweat, as my godfather's blue Mercedes driven by two young loyalists tore through the Lagos streets. Though tempted to read it, I knew not to violate an intimacy forged by time and war.

"They know this car," said the driver, as they pulled past policemen at the beginning of the Third Mainland Bridge. Due to the very late hour, the roads were free of the city's legendary traffic and we were moving at nightmare speed. "They fear this car, *abi*."

"It is true," the other concurred. "They fear this car and they should because it is his car. As long as they fear him, we are all okay."

They returned me to the home of one of my uncles in Lagos where I was staying. It was on Allen Avenue, an area then popular among the drug barons who'd made Nigeria a transshipment point for the global trade in narcotics. The streets were lined with prostitutes and late-night beer parlors, gambling dens, and a few nightclubs.

I could hear raucous laughter, clinking bottles, and loud arguments in the house. Electricity was out in the city, and I didn't hear a generator so it would be unbearable inside. I had no interest in confronting drunk drug barons lit up on Indian hemp — not

without AC. I thought to walk up to the main road to a beer parlor where I could buy a round of drinks for whomever was there
and have them fill my ears with stories. Instead, I decided to have
another cigarette and wait outside for the electricity to come on.

When I flicked the cigarette butt onto the ground, the gateman
emerged from the shadows to rescue it as if it were a coin. He
desperately pulled what he could of the remaining smoke into his
lungs. I went to him and gave him a fresh cigarette.

"*Oga,* thank you. Thank you."

"It's okay," I said, happy for a conversation.

"You know I knew your father."

It wasn't that I didn't believe him, but I tensed slightly, waiting
for the inevitable expression of entitlement, the request for beer,
food, clothing, betrothals to unseen daughters, or American visas.

As if he could read my suspicion in the dark, he quickly said,
"Yes, I was in the air force during the war. BAF1 was his car. I
remember it. BAF1."

"Yes, that was the license plate."

"He was very handsome. You do not look like him, but you
remind me of him."

I asked if he remembered my mother.

"Yes, *Oga*. The English woman."

"She was Jamaican, actually."

"I only know she was English and very strong. We saw her a lot when she came to see him at Uli where we were stationed. Seeing them together was a hopeful thing. Is she somewhere?"

"In America."

"That is where you are both living?"

"Yes, that's where we live."

"God is great. She should be in comfort. What of your sister?"

I looked at him quizzically.

"The one he had with the Onitsha woman," he said.

"I don't have a sister. I'm an only child."

He looked at me for a long moment and finished his cigarette. He seemed to have more to say and I kept waiting for him to speak. But then I was grateful he didn't and we smoked in silence.

I gave him another cigarette.

"Your father was handsome. You look just like him. He could have been president. Governor would be too small. The ones we have now are a problem. People like you scattered by war must come back. Only people like you can fix this place. If you came back, people in the East would vote for you. Eze Nd'Igbo would support you."

"I actually just came back from seeing Ojukwu. That was his car."

"Yes, I know the car," he said. "Everyone knows the car."

My cigarette was finished and I feared throwing the butt on the ground.

"*Oga,* tell me if you need anything," he said. "If you want a girl, I can bring her. I will bring her behind the kitchen. There is a small room there."

Then he was covered in dark at the threshold to the shack by the gate. His shadows became even darker as the electricity came on and the city shuddered into life again. I walked toward the house steeling myself for what I would find inside. It was unlikely I'd get much sleep, but I'd gotten used to it. The mosquitoes had either stopped biting me or I'd stopped paying attention to them. I was leaving tomorrow night, so before reaching the door to the kitchen, I went back and gave him the entire pack of cigarettes and the lighter. His mouth opened in surprise.

"Thank you, Big Brother. God will bless you."

His eyes were wet with tears.

12

The Man Who Fell to Earth

What I missed most about Nigeria once I was back in LA was a particular mantra that had kept me oriented. When the electricity went out, and the mosquitos descended, and the pressures of family history overwhelmed me, I told myself, *This will only make sense when I go back to America.* Of course, it didn't. And the reverse idea — that going to Africa would solve my problems with America — was proof of nothing more than how much of a Black American I'd become.

As an immigrant, I recognized exquisitely by now the limitations of race in the country I had grown up in. But this was the country where I'd formed the questions that had led me between and among dialects, cultures, and communities; and despite its own limitations, the academic world still seemed the best place to continue asking them. I'd never been like some of my aunts and uncles who'd counseled me and my cousins to leave the issue of race alone because it wasn't our business. As Great-Uncle Irving used to say, *We're here to drink the milk, not fuck with the cows.*

I chose to fuck with the cows. My first formal experience of doing that was with my dissertation topic, which drew harsh criticism and rejection by the few African American professors in my department and by white professors afraid to contradict them. They were angered by my desire to study the histories and outcomes of Black immigrants in this country, particularly as they differed from those of African Americans. They didn't want to sponsor a dissertation that described how and speculated why Black immigrants seemed at times to perform in America like many other immigrant groups and argued for how their different responses to racial prejudice influenced these outcomes. For many of these professors and my fellow students it was also a betrayal to make public the prejudices and tensions within Black communities. Turns out that Cousin Brian was right; there was only one story that mattered here.

I'd assumed that there was much to learn from the spaces among multiple Black stories, and about America's past and future in a world fast outgrowing this country's static racial categories. And that there was much these groups could teach one another about different approaches to racism, especially since so many Blacks from Africa and other places had been arriving in the United States in record numbers over the course of my own lifetime and were redefining Blackness in America. But for many of my professors and peers, the topic itself was taboo. The African American / white model was sacred. To stray too far from it was alien and dangerous. I decided to go elsewhere for advisors, which was seen as an act of treason. For me, it was just like high school when I was accused of snitching on my homies who'd stolen the sports equipment. I was always selling someone out.

I may have felt momentarily like both martyr and revolutionary for taking a stand, but changing professors took its toll. I was still one of the very few Blacks at that university at that level, and was even more isolated from my graduate peers than before. The space between Inglewood and the university now seemed farther than the distance I'd traveled to America in the first place. In the wake of the LA riots and the heartbreak that seemed to prefigure the violence, I could understand how easy it was for others to think about this country only in black and white terms and be uninterested in the differences and tensions within Blackness itself. After all, unpleasant run-ins with the police, which had in part fueled the riots, had been as much a part of my life as they were for any Black man growing up in Inglewood or South Central whether he went to college or not or had been born here or not. So when I received a job offer completely on the other side of the country, I took it even though it meant leaving my mother, uncles, aunts, and cousins in a neighborhood with walls still covered with soot from those nights of burning.

Academic life may have surrounded me with the luxury of ideas and the comfort of strangers, but it also caused me to move from school to school, job to job, coast to coast for some years, a perpetual migrant, unable or unwilling to claim anything as my own but books, theories, music, and memories. But just as I thought I'd gotten used to this kind of life — always leaving, always arriving, preferring to always be a stranger — I learned that my godfather had died.

I was preparing notes for a lecture or a class on Black diaspora, most likely. It was Thanksgiving Day. News of my godfather's death was squeezed at the bottom of the television screen below commercials heralding department store sales all over America. I'd initially read about his death on a Facebook posting by one of my young cousins in Nigeria, but I didn't take the news seriously until CNN confirmed it. Just three months before, the Nigerian press had been aflutter with tales of his demise. For a time, it seemed as if he were always dying and coming back to life, always in exile and always returning. Neither these rehearsals nor the fact that I knew he'd been unwell for some time cushioned the shock of my godfather's death. When the news came, my life adrift suddenly became intolerable.

In the emotionally difficult days following, I found myself turning to a memory of landfall, of home, of my godfather, but not in Nigeria. I was suddenly missing LA where he had visited before I'd started thinking about Africa as a possible solution to questions I hadn't yet formulated. I'd recently returned from Jamaica where my head had been split open. The past had become dangerous to contemplate. He arrived at our house without security or entourage, and I remember being initially unimpressed. He wasn't dressed like a general or a warlord or the son of Africa's first millionaire or an Oxford-educated playboy or a former head of state. He looked like any uncle arriving to spend a few days in sunny California. Sandals even. He carried himself with an elegant self-confidence my friends would have called effeminate. The way he moved suggested that fame was even more liberating than I'd dreamed. It took me hours to feel confident enough to speak to him though he constantly looked at me, made eye contact, as if he had a secret to share. When my mother was at work, he and I spent the days together, talking, walking, watching television, and more talking. He was the most well-read Black person

I'd ever met and loved books without apology or justification. He even did something I'd always dreamed of doing: he quoted books and poems in conversation—loudly.

I took him through the streets of our neighborhood, down La Brea and deep into Inglewood, but also in the other direction to the park in the middle of the Crenshaw District where African cultural festivals were held in the summer and Rastafarians dotted the landscape. This was near Great-Uncle Irving's house, which I showed him along with the Jamaican restaurant that bore my mother's maiden name. He taught me to throw a knife in our backyard. We used an empty shoebox as a target. When I failed to achieve the heroic overhand throw á la karate movies or adventure novels, he showed me how much more accurate it was to throw the knife underhand. Also effeminate, I thought, but definitely more lethal.

I had no idea what to talk to him about so I told him about the Diamond Dogs and what it was like to move through a world structured by gangs, the police, and athletic teams. I boasted a bit too much, especially when I was hailed by the boys on the street. Maybe I thought proximity to the violence of our neighborhood made me worthy of my legacy. After all, he'd led an army and fought a war. I'd been seeing images of that war my whole life, of him and my father standing next to men who would become leaders of other African countries and who I'd next encounter in books in my college classes.

I think I wanted him to marry my mother. That would somehow have been appropriate. For some reason, I believed that my father would have sanctioned it, and it would have freed me from the ever-present sense that my mother existed solely for me.

My godfather visited for only a few days, but he was able to come to Aunt Pansy and Uncle Owen's house for lunch after church one Sunday. He had to: he was a hero to all of the elders in our immigrant community, even Great-Uncle Irving who, despite his hostility to all things Biafra or Nigeria, did have a weakness for celebrity. It was a full house that Sunday. Everyone and everywhere was there, especially Nigerians and other West Africans, and the accents and dialects were at a pitch and intensity I'd never heard before, not even for Independence Day celebrations.

I remember that my Yoruba Aunt Joy was in tears the whole time. Even her husband showed up, not with his official wife of course, but he did wear his chief's robes and hat and carried the straw fan titled men carried for ceremonial occasions. And their son didn't say "nigger" once. I remember a few aunts came straight from work, wearing their blue or white nursing costumes. Others were in full traditional West African regalia, the colors blinding. There were people I hadn't seen in years, some I'd never seen before, and those I wouldn't see again. My godfather was seated at the head of the dining table, and for the first time, I saw Uncle Owen act like a house boy, running back and forth to the kitchen to fill my godfather's cup or replace a dropped fork or chide one of the baffled young cousins who wanted to know if this was the same South African gentleman who ran the dry cleaners on La Brea Avenue, and if not, whose freedom were we celebrating now?

My godfather may have been the guest of honor, but I was in my glory because he sat me on his right and held my hand for the whole time and continued making eye contact with me, suggesting that this intimacy between us was in fact the message he had come to convey. Uncle Owen must have noticed because he filled my cup too, picked up my dropped utensils, and, most important, listened when I talked. Everyone did. Someone would rush to the turntable to put on whatever music I wanted to hear. My mother was seated on my godfather's left. Though she wasn't in traditional Nigerian garb, she looked glamorous and regal to me, the way she'd always been described by those who knew her before America and the way she appeared in the black-and-white photos stuffed in boxes under our couch.

At a certain point when the music and the conversation had grown particularly loud, I heard my godfather say, "This was the dream. Africa, the Middle Passage, and the New World, all at once. That is what we were fighting for. Quite so. The pan-African dream."

I felt he was talking to me specifically since I was the one who was all of those things at once and who had suffered for being so. He couldn't have been talking about the people at the table so full of arguments and fighting, dramatic standoffs and painful judgments. Belonging to this was to be bruised always by it, to feel always as if you were failing it. The young ones were fighting over the stereo, the music loud and rude and abrupt in moving from calypso to reggae, high life to rhythm and blues with no justification. Aunt Pansy broke into rooms upstairs to make sure the teenage male and female cousins remembered that we were related by blood even if we mostly weren't. Was that marijuana smoke on the patio? Aunties were screaming at uncles who could only respond by asserting a power that the women believed they allowed the men to hold in the first place. Eyes would roll and necks would snap. There was a lot of goat meat and enough curry for the smell to stick to everyone's skin for days. My godfather was ecstatic, glorying in it all.

My mother sat on the other side of him, beatific, and I again hoped they'd get married, not for their sakes but for mine. If I couldn't be king of Black America, then I could be prince of the dining table.

* * *

The cousin who'd posted the information about my godfather's death on Facebook had been stationed in Northern Nigeria for his yearlong stint of National Youth Service. He'd been there during the initial waves of vicious anti-Christian pogroms in the North led by the fundamentalist movement, Boko Haram —a Hausa phrase meaning "Western education is sacrilege." For months before my godfather's death, that group had been bombing churches, opening fire on markets, and massacring Nigerians from the Southern ethnic groups as well as less orthodox Muslims. My cousins in the North kept me apprised of the family's safety on Facebook, huddling in Internet cafés between power outages or sending random phone texts when the network was up. The pogroms had brought Biafra back into public memory.

Not that Biafra was ever far from the surface in Nigeria. These acts of violence made my godfather's death more poignant, especially as the various ethnic groups began to talk of reprisal killings. Some of my cousins in the East had boasted that people had already begun doing just that, picking off herders in the Hausa cattle village that skirted the edge of Onitsha and smothering a few with burning tires, an old staple of native justice. The southern delta of the Niger River had been for years rife with kidnappings and uprisings over the grossly unevenly distributed oil economy. This unrest also resonated with my godfather's death. This was also when a new Biafra movement began to make the international news after growing beneath public awareness for a number of years.

But instead of Nigerian politics, the news led me to thinking about my mother. Since I was a teenager, she'd been making me promise to return her remains to Nigeria even though everyone in our family expected her to be buried in Jamaica, or in America where her son, the Black American, was clearly going to spend his life. As the cancer grew to consume her, she'd intensified this request, reminding me of it regularly even as I spent most of my time and effort promising her I would while believing she would survive simply because she'd already survived so much.

She died, however, just after I'd gotten tenure, weeks before my first book was published. I was happy that she was able at least to see the dedication to her, which I read through the rumble of the life-sustaining machines attached to her body.

The last time I'd seen my godfather was when I took her remains back to Nigeria for burial. We'd waited for him at our compound, holding off the dozens of people who remembered my mother and father from the war and the very many more who'd heard that the King of the Igbos was expected to preside over the ceremony. Eventually, we went ahead with the burial, placing my mother's remains next to my father's grave near the house he'd built for her before the war scattered us.

We found out later that my godfather had collapsed the day

before while visiting a church outside of Onitsha and had been hospitalized. When he and I later spoke on the phone, he told me I should be proud. I'd done my duty and reunited my mother and my father. I reminded him that according to village custom my father was still alive since I still had to arrange the appropriate rites, which given my father's stature would take time and money. He said my father's spirit had been waiting for nothing more than to witness her return. This completed their story, he said. Everything else was mine now.

Those two deaths sealed the loss of the sense of heroic mission I'd carried since childhood. I felt now only the exhaustion that came from relentless movement and the nostalgia that came from having left too many places without knowing any of them well enough to call them home. The deaths left me, however, with a gift, the memory of my mother and my godfather at Aunt Pansy and Uncle Owen's house. Maybe it was a way of managing loss, but I began to think of my godfather's dream at the dining table as the lesson that I'd expected to get from him when I visited him in Lagos years ago. He'd already shared it with me, it just took me all this time and loss to grow into it. Because the dream was big, so expansive that it needed a place big enough to hold it. My godfather had seen the dream in Inglewood, California, east of LAX and the Pacific Ocean but well south of Hollywood or Beverly Hills or those other places that signify Los Angeles to most people. It was a place, after all, big enough for everything my mother and I had brought with us and everything we'd left behind but still carried, and for all the stuff that remained boxed up and stored under couches. Big enough eventually to remake our expectations of this country and of each other, and to allow us to hide from the responsibility of having had those expectations in the first place. What my godfather was celebrating was fractious and painful. But any attempt to render that dream as unified or the possession of any one people or voice would lead to failure, tragedy, violence. I didn't have to fight a war or start a country to learn that.

By the time the name and face of General Chukwuemeka Odumegwu Ojukwu had vanished from the television screen along with the accompanying black-and-white images of children stricken with kwashiorkor, and as the news shifted to the civil wars of department store Black Friday sales, my arrival in America all those years ago seemed if not fated then at least inevitable. The scars and bruises I carried were because I'd fallen to earth and had landed in a country where I could fulfill the promise of my true name.

Acknowledgments

As always, there's too much to say and too little space and time, too many to thank for their contribution to the opportunity and very ability to tell this tale. There are names, however, that must appear at the end of these pages.

Deanne Urmy, for seeing what I didn't see despite or perhaps because of my having lived with it for so long. Jill Kneerim, for relentless advocacy and an understanding of scope and scale. Kristin Lawless, for reciprocity. And Onyi, for roots after a lifetime of errancy.

Women have truly shaped my diaspora.